HUSBANDS BY DESIGN

Endorsements

Pastor Ed Johnson III does a remarkable job dealing with the God-given role of the husband in the institution of marriage. This book is a must-read for all married men as well as those planning to become husbands in the future.

Dr. Karry D. Wesley, *Senior Pastor*
Antioch Fellowship Missionary Baptist Church (Dallas, TX)
www.afmbc.org

With an engaging style, written almost like a personal conversation, Ed Johnson III lays out a biblical charge to husbands to be all that God intends them to be in Jesus Christ. Honest and direct with a touch of humor, this book provides a brief but thorough look at the wisdom of God's design for husbands and how they can glorify Christ by loving their wives.

Gary Cook, *President*
Dallas Baptist University
www.dbu.edu

Husbands by Design is a work that reaches up to the Father while simultaneously speaking across the spectrum to husbands who are newlywed and seasoned pros in this married life. EJ has penned a playbook that is both theologically sound and everyday applicable. Both husbands and husbands-to-be will find nuggets of great value and worth in these pages.

C.M. Pearl Winslow, *Program Manager*
The Urban Alternative (National Ministry of Dr. Tony Evans)
www.tonyevans.org

I recommend this book to men who accept the privilege of being husbands. Ed provides clear instruction and inspiration for married men.

James R. Womack, M.H.S.A., Th.M.
Lead Pastor, Destiny Church
www.discoverdestiny.org

The question that God asked in the Garden, "Adam, where are you?" still rings loud and true today. However, like soldiers and leaders, men become fathers and husbands by training and development. In Husbands by Design, Ed Johnson III provides a practical, biblical, and challenging training manual to equip men to becoming the godly husbands and fathers designed by God.

Dr. Maurice Pugh, Senior Pastor
New Life Fellowship Church
www.nlifefellowship.org

Ed has done a phenomenal job merging both the truths of Scripture with the realities of married life. He addresses husbands in a contemporary and engaging way that causes husbands to lean in to what he has to say. Every man needs to pick up this book to better understand and maximize this important God given role. As a husband, I have been challenged and inspired by, Husbands by Design and you will too.

Bryan Carter, Senior Pastor
Concord Church (Dallas, TX)
www.concorddallas.org

The daily challenges for Christian households are great, and when the focus is upon the Christian husband, even greater. The struggle to serve our wives and families with passion and excellence can seem impossible, especially when the struggles outside the home seem equally as great. Ed Johnson III shines a bright light into the darkened crevices of the Christian husband's heart; his fears, struggles, and longings. He identifies many of those "blind spots" that have destroyed the marriages of many Believers, and with scriptural and spiritual clarity, Ed offers hope. Hope that we can overcome. Hope that we can make God proud. Hope that we can honor God with a godly marriage. Husbands, this is the book you've longed to read.

Stephen G. Brown, *Pastor/Servant Leader*
Greater Bethlehem Baptist Church (Dallas, TX)
www.greaterdallas.org

HUSBANDS BY DESIGN

A Biblical Blueprint of Godly Husbands

ED JOHNSON III

LUCIDBOOKS

Husbands by Design: A Biblical Blueprint of Godly Husbands

© Ed Johnson III

Published by Lucid Books in Houston, TX.

www.LucidBooks.net

ISBN 10: 1632960338
ISBN 13: 978-1-63296-033-7
eISBN 10: 1632960346
eISBN 13: 978-1-63296-034-4

Special Sales: Most Lucid Books titles are available in special quantity discounts. Custom imprinting or excerpting can also be done to fit special needs. Contact Lucid Books at info@lucidbooks.net.

Unless otherwise noted, all references to Scripture are taken from the English Standard Version of the Bible.

Dedication

To my wife who has been and continues to be instrumental in helping me to grow into a Christ-centered, godly husband: Thanks for loving me in spite of me, and being patient as our Heavenly Father builds me into a man and a husband who reflects Jesus in all of life.

Table of Contents

Introduction

The date was Saturday, May 18, 2002. A scrawny 25 year old stood at the front of a church eagerly awaiting the entrance of his bride. The ushers placed down the aisle runner. The flower girls littered it with rose petals. And then the moment he – and everyone in attendance – was waiting for finally arrived. "Will everyone please rise," said the officiating minister. And on cue, the ushers slowly opened the door and there she was; my radiant fiancée dressed in an elegant wedding gown being escorted by her father. About thirty minutes or so later, the wedding was over and the marriage had begun.

As I look back to that day, I thank God for how he prepared me to step into the role of being a husband: from my late father's example to the pre-marital classes, book reading assignments, and counseling sessions. It was all tremendously helpful. But it is one thing to study game footage; it is quite another when you actually step onto the court. Out of all the prep work I put in going into marriage, I still had much to learn and a whole lot of maturing to do. With twelve years now under my belt, gratefully, by God's grace, I can say I've grown since those honeymoon years.

But does a little over a decade of marriage experience qualify me to write such a book? Well, that depends on who you ask. For those who have been married the same amount of years as me or less, would probably say "yes." To those who have been married longer, their answer would probably be "no." What follows in this book, however, is not content based primarily on what I have to say about being a husband from my own marriage (although I do of course, at points, use my marriage as an illustration), but more so a study of what the Bible teaches on the subject and matters related to it.

Why a book solely directed to Christian husbands? Why not a book on marriage in general that addresses both husbands and wives? There are a number of reasons, but let me just state two. One, if we as husbands are the point leaders in our marriages, then I believe instruction, responsibility and accountability needs to begin with us. And two, having served as one of the staff pastors at my church now for 10 years and conducted numerous pre-marital and marital counseling sessions, I have seen brothers in the Lord struggle and limp along in their understanding and execution of their role as husbands and I simply wanted to lend a helping hand by writing a book on the Book that would encourage, enlighten, challenge, and strengthen them, as well as affirm those who are doing well.

Additionally, though my target audience is married Christian men, I believe this book will even be useful for those men who are single but looking to be married one day; a training guide of sorts, if you will.

Godly husbands are not born; they are made. Divinely made by the Father in Christ, through the Spirit, and according to the Bible. We are husbands by design. Let's take a look at the biblical blueprint and get to work.

Chapter 1

Don't Be A Jerk! Be Like Jesus to Her

T hey both were in their mid-20's; just young and "wet behind the ears" (an idiom which means inexperienced, naïve, and/or immature), as my late father would say. They had only been married a short while, but their relationship was already on the rocks. A member of our church, who knew them personally, recommended that they contact me to see if I could help them with their marital issues. They were not members of our church, but that didn't matter because I just wanted to help salvage their marriage. So we scheduled a time for them to come by my office to begin marriage counseling. If I recall correctly, I don't think we even made it past two sessions before they, or more accurately, he, decided not to continue any further. Here's the gist of what happened (Please note that the names of the couple and the details of their lives have all been changed for confidentiality purposes.):

Me: "Hey guys. So, tell me what's going on with you two."

Janet: "I'm just tired of being upset and crying all the time, especially when it just seems like he doesn't care."

Me: "Can you elaborate a little more on why you feel that way, Janet?"

Janet: "It's just…" (She stops speaking to keep from emotionally breaking down.)

Me: "It's okay, Janet. Take your time."

Jamal: "Well, I'll tell you because it probably has something to do with me anyway."

Me: "Okay, go ahead, Jamal. But I want to come back to your wife to see what she has to say."

Jamal: "She's probably all upset because I travel a lot, so I am barely at home. And when I am, you know, I gotta stay on my grind to make that paper." (Translation: I have to keep working to make money.)

Janet: "It's not just that, Jamal, and you know it!"

Jamal: "Know what?!"

Me: "Hold on, Jamal. Just let her talk."

Janet: "Don't get me wrong, Pastor Johnson, I knew before we got married that he was going to be on the road quite a bit. But then we had children and I thought he would do the right thing and try to cut back some so that he could be home more to help me. But what really got me was the women."

Me: "Women? What do you mean?"

Janet: "Apparently, a part of his job includes going to parties with women, hanging out, drinking, and 'dancing' with them.

I've tried to talk with him about this – about how it makes me uncomfortable, about how it hurts me to know that I am at home taking care of the kids while he is away meeting different women in every city he goes to. But every time I do he gets upset." (She starts to cry.)

Me: "Is that true, Jamal?"

Jamal: "Yeah, it's true. But listen, it's what I have to do. And she knows it. She knew this when we met and eloped in Las Vegas that day, and I told her what line of work I was in."

Me: ... (A huge red flag goes up in my mind.)

Janet: "Yes I knew what type of work you did, but I didn't know that you and these women would be all up on each other. As I told you before, I don't like it and it makes me very uncomfortable and insecure in our marriage."

Jamal: "Yeah, well, if I'm going to make it big in this business, I've got to do what I've got to do."

Me: "Okay, Jamal. But do you hear what your wife is saying to you; that she is uncomfortable with this job situation and that it is causing her to be insecure in your marriage?"

Jamal: "Yeah I hear her, but, listen, I am not going to change. I am trying to make it big in this industry. She needs to just chill. I am doing this for her and our kids."

Me: "But Jamal, some things are not worth pursuing or holding on to if they are going to damage your marriage. Wouldn't you agree?"

Jamal: "Let me just shoot straight with you. I am not going to stop what I am doing. I am trying to be the best in the biz. So, I am going to do what I have to do to make it to the top. She's just going to have to deal with it."

Janet: "See, he just doesn't care about me or how I feel."

Me: "Jamal, your wife is obviously in a lot of anguish concerning your choices. If you are going to salvage this marriage, *you* are going to have make some changes."

Jamal: "I don't know what else to say to you or to her. I am not going to stop what I am doing. Period."

Me: "Well, unfortunately if that is your attitude and approach to this, then I am not going to be much help to you. So to not waste any more of your time or mine, I think this will be our last session together because it is obvious, now that we have been through a few of these, that you, Jamal, are not going to take seriously your wife's legitimate concerns regarding your decisions. I sincerely hope that you will have a change of heart. But for now, we are done. Please understand though that my door is always open. If things change, please don't hesitate to call me."

At that point, Jamal got up without a moment's hesitation, we shook hands, and he walked out with a despondent Janet in tow. I sat there for a few minutes, mulling over what I had just experienced and shaking my head in disbelief over the callousness of Jamal's heart towards his wife. He was inconsiderate and unfaithful to his wife, and selfish and egotistical in his pursuits. Jamal, to be frank, was simply acting like a jerk. But before we rush to castigate Jamal and exile him to deadbeat husband land by himself, consider this: we all have some "jerkish" ways about us. Do we not? All of us exhibit varying degrees of "jerkism" in our marriages, and deserve to spend some time on that island ourselves. My prayer is that, through this chapter, the Holy Spirit will inspire and empower us to be less like jerks and more like Jesus to our wives. The question becomes then: what does being more like Jesus to our wives entail?

THE MODEL FOR HUSBANDS

There are no perfect men (which consequently means that there are no perfect husbands either). Well, actually, there is one and his name is Jesus. Paul, in Ephesians 5:25ff, presents Jesus to us as the consummate man after whom we should pattern ourselves, particularly when it comes to how we ought to live and lead in relationship to our wives. According to this passage of Scripture, it is Christ's relationship to the Church that not only serves as the prototype for, but also the basis of, the mandate to us as Christian husbands. And, yes, I said *Christian* husbands because our reflection of Christ before our wives is only possible in and through a relationship with Christ; wherein we receive him, by faith, into our lives, and thereafter continually repent of our sin and submit to his lordship, which he exercises through the Word and the Holy Spirit. It is in him we are given new – and eternal – life; that is, a new nature: one that is free from the controlling power of sin, Satan, and the world's evil system and that is progressively becoming more righteous through the sanctifying work of the Holy Spirit as he brings the word of God to bear on our lives (2 Corinthians 5:17, 21; Romans 6; 2 Thessalonians 2:13; 2 Timothy 3:16). This is great news because no matter if you and I as men grew up in a traditional two-parent home and saw a great yet imperfect or bad example of a husband, or whether we were raised by a single parent and didn't see one at all, we can still become the kind of husbands that God desires by looking at Jesus and what he did for the Church.

So what does being and acting more like Jesus to our wives look like? Paul gives us one word, a command: Love. He writes, "Husbands, love your wives…" (Ephesians 5:25a). "Is that it?" you ask. I realize that you love your wives and probably tell them so on occasion or quite frequently. But, as many of you know, love is more than saying "I love you" or a feeling. The word for love here means, "To have a preference for, wish well to, regard the welfare of."[1] This kind of love goes beyond emotion or cognition; it is about demonstration. As Bruce Van Horn tweeted, "LOVE is a 4-letter verb!" And if there is anyone who epitomizes love it is God. Check out these passages of Scripture that speak of his love for us:

> "For God so loved the world that he **gave** his only begotten Son that whoever believes in him will not perish, but will have eternal life." (John 3:16, emphasis mine)

> "But God **shows** his love for us in that while we were still sinners Christ died for us." (Romans 5:8, emphasis mine)

> "In this the love of God was made **manifest** among us, that God sent his only Son into the world, so that we might live through him." (1 John 4:9, emphasis mine)

Paul, as a part of his directive, points us to the death of Jesus, which in essence shows and summarizes what it means to love our wives. He writes, "...as Christ loved the church and gave himself up for her," (Ephesians 5:25b, emphasis mine; cf. also, Galatians 2:20, Ephesians 5:2). The bold-faced phrase is a reference to Jesus' redemptive work on the cross for our sins. In this historical, one-time act we see, in an ultimate sense, what love is and are therefore able to understand what God expects of us in relationship to our wives on a continual basis. In verses 26 and 27, Paul gives two purposes for which Jesus gave up his life for the church: 1. That he might sanctify (to set apart for himself) her, and 2. That he might present the church to himself without spot or wrinkle or any such thing, with the resulting purpose that she might be holy and without blemish.

[1] Thayer, Joseph H. *Thayer's Greek-English Lexicon of the New Testament*. Grand Rapids: Baker Book House, 1977.

One could seek to apply these purposes that Christ brings about for the church to our relationship with our wives. To do so, I think, would be pressing the details of these verses too far; hence, causing us to miss the overall point – which is to love our wives like our own bodies as Christ does with his own body, the church (we will look at this in more detail in the next section of this chapter). Suffice it to say at this juncture that Paul is calling us to model Christ's love of the church to our spouses by voluntarily sacrificing ourselves for their benefit unto the glory of God, regardless of their actions. How this looks on a practical level will differ from marriage to marriage. But here are some general pointers to help you think about how you can apply this in your relationship.

Establish Your Priorities

Outside of your relationship with God, if I were to ask you where does your wife rank on your list of priorities, what would be your answer? Hopefully she would be number one. Not your family members. Not your friends, boys, or fraternity members. Not even your children. Genesis 2:24a says, "Therefore a man shall leave his father and his mother and hold fast to his wife..." What this means is that when you and I stood before the officiant, took those vows, and saluted our respective brides, at that moment our marriages became the primary and central human relationship of our lives. Everyone else revolves around them. I know all guys don't watch or play sports, but even if you are a casual fan of basketball you will understand this analogy: your wife shouldn't feel like the 6th man on the team, waiting for her turn to get on the court of life with you. She is the star player on your squad and should be treated as such. Have you given someone other than your wife the top spot in your life? If so, it's time to adjust your roster and minimize that person's minutes in your life, or maybe even bench him or her altogether.

Consider Jesus and how he prioritized us, the church, even on the night of his betrayal by Judas. You can sense the place we held in his heart during his life on earth (and yet still as he continues his ministry of intercession for us before the Father) as you read his high priestly prayer in the gospel according to John:

> "I have manifested your name to the people whom you gave me out of the world. Yours they were, and you gave them to me, and they have kept your word...I am praying for them. I am not praying for the world but for those whom you have given me, for they are yours...I do not ask for these only, but also for those who will believe in me through their word, that they may all be one, just as you, Father, are in me, and I in you, that they also may be in us, so that the world may believe that you sent me." (John 17:6, 9, 20-21)

Please don't misunderstand what I am saying. I am not communicating that we should slavishly cater to our wives to the wholesale neglect of other significant relationships. Should you still go to the family reunions and get-togethers at Big Mama's house, hang out with your frat or friends, or hit the golf course or the gym with your buddies? By all means, feel free. But in all of your decisions you should consider your wife; and be willing to adjust or suspend your time with those people for her, if necessary.

Leverage Your Power

It was a Thursday night. Jesus and the Twelve disciples were gathered together in a room, enjoying a supper before the Feast of the Passover. After some time, Jesus quietly and intentionally rose from the table, "laid aside his outer garments, and taking a towel, tied it around his waist. Then he poured water into a basin and began to wash the disciples' feet and to wipe them with the towel that was wrapped around him." (John 13:4-5). What an astounding act of service! It was so bewildering to Peter that he questioned and even objected to Jesus washing his feet (John 13:6, 8). Why did Peter do such a thing? The Bible Knowledge Commentary sheds some light on the backdrop of this text, enabling us to understand the mental disequilibrium Peter experienced as he saw Jesus approach him to wash his feet:

> "Foot-washing was needed in Palestine. The streets were dusty and people wore sandals without socks or stockings. It was a mark of honor for a host to provide a servant to wash a guest's feet; it was a breach of hospitality not to provide for it (cf. 1 Sam. 25:41; Luke 7:40-50; 1 Tim. 5:10). Wives often washed their husbands' feet, and children washed their parents' feet. Most people, of course, had to wash their own feet." (pg. 320)[2]

This act of washing feet was also seen as menial, a task that was to be performed by a servant, never a master. Jesus inverted this whole concept. Instead of the servants washing the master's feet, the master washes theirs. Pay careful attention to what Jesus said to the disciples after he finished,

> "You call me Teacher and Lord, and you are right, for so I am. If I then, your Lord and Teacher, have washed your feet, you also ought to wash one another's feet. For I have given you an example, that you also should do just as I have done to you. Truly, truly, I say to you, a servant is not greater than his master, nor is a messenger greater than the one who sent him." (John 13:13-16)

---

[2] John F. Walvoord and Roy B. Zuck, eds., *The Bible Knowledge Commentary (New Testament Edition)*. Colorado Springs: Cook Communication Ministries, 1983, 2004.

As husbands then, Jesus expects us to exemplify servant leadership to our wives, willingly and joyfully leveraging our headship, leadership, or power (in the sense of authority) for their benefit. Christ-centered, husband-leaders primarily look to serve, not be served. Servant leadership is selfless leadership. Instead of guarding our title, we need to grab a towel and wash our wives' feet. You fix her plate sometimes. Iron her work clothes. Watch the kids, so that she can have some personal time. Periodically interrupt whatever her routine acts of service are to you and the home and do it yourself, or secure the services of someone else to take care of it, if you are unable. Wash her feet and it will encourage her to walk in sync with you and towards you, rather than away from you.

Dismiss Your Prerogatives

After supper, Jesus journeyed with his disciples to the Mount of Olives, to a place called Gethsemane. He took Peter, James, and John aside with him and had the other disciples to sit and wait while he went to pray. At a point Jesus went a little further away from his inner circle, fell on his face in deep anguish and prayed, "My Father, if it be possible, let this cup pass from me…" (Matthew 26:39b). What is this cup imagery? "For biblical writers, what gives a cup significance is not its appearance but its contents. A cup may hold a blessing – liquid that sustains life, quenches thirst, engenders fellowship – or it may hold a curse—liquid that induces drunkenness or even death." (Dictionary of Biblical Imagery, pg. 186[3]). In the Old Testament, a cup was predominately used to symbolize God's wrath and judgment against sin (Isaiah 51:17; Jeremiah 25:15-16). Given this information and the context of Jesus' prayer, it becomes clear what Jesus meant when he employed this cup imagery. It was the full cup of the righteous judgment of God

---

[3] Leland Ryken, et. al., *Dictionary of Biblical Imagery.* Downers Grove: InterVarsity Press, 1998.

against our sins that he was to consume on the cross of Calvary. He who knew no sin would become sin to deliver those in sin through his sacrificial, substitutionary death. Jesus would die in the place of sinners. This is the cup that Jesus, in a moment of genuine human vulnerability, prayed might pass from him. But what is astonishing is Jesus' statement at the end of his prayer, "nevertheless, not as I will, but as you will." (Matthew 26:39c) In the face of an impending, unimaginable, agonizing death for sinful humanity, Jesus laid aside his desire in order to fulfill his Heavenly Father's will of providing salvation to mankind.

As men who seek to model our lives after Jesus, this is the type of loving sacrifice that ought to characterize our headship; a sacrifice which says that we are willing – though we may struggle with it at times – to dismiss our prerogatives for our wives' good. And, yes, this often times is uncomfortable and feels like you are dying. That's to be expected when you seek to live a cruciform life. Marriage is a life-long march up to Calvary's hill where we die daily to ourselves for our wives. The way of life in our marriages is the way of death. We die to our will and submit to the Father's will as it concerns our wives. In our marriages, our primary focus should be on bearing crosses as husband-servants rather than wearing crowns as husband-kings—i.e., becoming twistedly enamored with our position of leadership and thus misusing it like a deranged dictator who is consumed by power and seeks to satisfy his selfish desires to the detriment of those under his tyrannical rule.

Defer Your Plans

To sacrifice for our wives doesn't always mean that we must totally give up the things that we like, or hope to do or achieve. In many cases, it is more about putting off for a time our pursuits, so that they can be about theirs. So, for example, say you have a child or two. If your wife wants to take a class to further herself educationally at the same time you normally head to the park to play ball, then consider staying at home to watch the kids and go at a later time.

I can distinctly recall one instance when I had to put this into practice in our marriage. I had thoughts of immediately pursuing my doctorate after completing my Master of Divinity degree. It had been an aspiration of mine, and I had every intent on fulfilling it, at least at the outset of me pondering the idea. As it turned out, after graduating, I wasn't absolutely sure what direction I wanted to go in. I thought to myself, "Should I go get a Ph.D. or a Doctor of Ministry degree?" Some years passed and it was tabled. And then one day my wife came to me and said she would really like to go back to school to get her MBA. Now although my educational aspiration had been on hold for a couple of years due to my ambivalence, at that moment, I could have said, "Baby, although it has been a minute, you know early on I was thinking of going to get my doctorate after my masters. Though I am still not certain at this point, I would like for you to wait until I can make up my mind as to what I want to do. So, let me figure out my plan first and then we will get to yours." That would have been selfish of me, contrary to a Christ-like sacrificial love. But, by God's grace, I chose to look out for her interests and not merely my own.

Now anything can be taken to an extreme. I am by no means implying that as husbands we should placate to every wish or whim of our wives (and neither should they with us, by the way). But when our wives present to us a legitimate, beneficial and important opportunity for them—which usually has positive effects in our marriages and families—that conflicts with our own, we need to give serious thought and prayer to deferring our plans.

Utilize Your Possessions

There was much I admired and appreciated about my late father: his devotion to Jesus, his character, his insatiable desire to learn, his dedication to one church for life, and his discipline, just to name a few. One that stands out as well was his loyalty to, and love for, his wife until his passing. One way that he displayed that love was his day-to-day decision to work hard and live simply to ensure that my mother had everything she needed as well as some things she wanted. My father told me on occasion that he didn't want much in the way of clothes, cars, or electronics because, for one, he was content with the basic necessities of life, but also because he wanted to utilize what he had to care for my mother. He lived such a modest lifestyle that my mom would take it upon herself to go shopping for him so that he would have some new clothes and work uniforms. If she didn't do this, she knew he would take care of what he had until it just became an absolute necessity for him to get some more. He just didn't believe in living such an extravagant lifestyle to the point where his wife went without or to where they had no financial margin. He was always thinking about her when it came to the finances and other assets. After coming to understand that his cancer was terminal, he, by God's grace, didn't use his mortality as an excuse to live riotously. As a matter of fact, that only seemed to bolster his commitment to provide for my mom. He made sure that her name was on every account, including his business. She was the primary beneficiary on his life insurance. He sold his work truck and all his tools, so she wouldn't have to bother with it when he was gone. He made sure all of the appliances were in tip top shape to prevent her from being hit with repair costs, at least for a while, or having to buy new ones. He even had the foresight to trade in her car for a more manageable one, seeing that she would soon be a widow and didn't need the headache of trying to maintain it. Now that's servant leadership.

But there is an even better example of this point. The best example to be exact. God. He spared no "expense" to save us spiritually. What did it cost God the Father to redeem us? His Son, Jesus—"He who did not spare his own Son but gave him up for us all, how will he not also with him graciously give us all things?" (Romans 8:32). The least we can do is to show that same type of love to our wives materially.

Own Your Problems

Clearly, this point doesn't apply to Jesus—because he had no problems to own up to or sins to confess; he was sinless and perfect in all his ways (2 Corinthians 5:21; Hebrews 4:15)—but it does to us. We all cause and bring problems into our marriages. They can be immoral (e.g. lying to our wives), or innocent or idiosyncratic (e.g. forgetting to turn the outside lights on at night for your wife before she comes home, or leaving your dirty shirt on the bed instead of putting it in the laundry basket) in nature. When we are faced with our sinful or poor decisions, we need to pray and ask God to help us to not pull an Adam: blaming our wives rather than first owning up to what we did (see Genesis 3:11-12). Whether we are partly or wholly the culprits behind our marital issues, we must *humbly* take ownership of our actions, confessing and, if at all possible, correcting them. Holy and humble husbands don't deny personal and moral shortcomings; we shoulder them and proceed, like King David in Psalm 51, to the throne of God in prayer to seek forgiveness and cleansing from our unrighteousness, and sincerely apologize to our wives.

ONE FLESH

When you study verses 25 through 27, in light of the entire passage, of Ephesians chapter five verses 22 through 33, I believe Paul's overall point is not for us to exactly replicate the purposes that Christ uniquely carries out in relationship to the church, but rather to love our wives, who are a part of the "one flesh" marital union with us, in the same way as Christ does for his body, the church. This one flesh or body motif runs throughout this section of Scripture. Paul employs it five times: vs. 23—"his body," vs. 28—"as their own bodies," vs. 29—"his own flesh," vs. 30—"his body," and vs. 31—"one flesh." We are to love our wives, Paul says, as our own bodies, for in loving them we are loving ourselves because they are one flesh with us. In verse 29, we are given two aspects of loving our wives as our own bodies.

We Nourish Them

The word nourish means to nurture or bring up. When applied to children, the idea is to nurture or bring them up to maturity. Now of course our wives are not our children and should, therefore, not be viewed nor related to as such. But what this does mean—keeping in mind the thread of the one flesh or body image that is woven throughout this entire section of Scripture—is that they should grow and flourish under our loving care and leadership.

We are to nourish them spiritually. Obviously, if our wives are Christians, they have a personal responsibility to grow in the grace and knowledge of the Lord Jesus. But you and I can play a part in that by doing things that will encourage their spiritual growth. We can pray for and, yes, even with them (which might seem awkward and maybe even scary to us at first, but if they are maturing believers in Jesus, they will appreciate us taking the initiative). Willingly and gladly attending church, marriage classes, retreats or conferences, or reading and discussing the Scriptures with them, buying them solid Christian books, and encouraging them to participate in the discipleship gatherings (e.g., small groups, Sunday School, Bible classes, etc.) at our churches are just some of the ways we can encourage them to grow in their relationship with God.

We are to nourish them relationally. In his book, *Five Love Languages: How to Express Heartfelt Commitment to Your Mate*[4],

---

[4] Gary D. Chapman, *The Five Love Languages: How to Express Heartfelt Commitment to Your Mate*. Chicago: Northfield Publishing, 2004

Dr. Gary Chapman gives five ways to communicate love to your spouse in a way that she (or he for the wives) will understand it. Your spouse possesses one or any mix of the following love languages: Words of Affirmation, Gifts, Acts of Service, Physical Touch, and Quality Time. I have read this book and happen to agree with Dr. Chapman's thesis. I recommend you purchase a copy and read it for yourself. I trust it will be a blessing to your marriage as it has been in mine. Having said that, I believe there is one love language that applies to every one of our wives—and to ourselves as well–because it is a basic component of being in a relationship with someone: quality time. This is fundamental to you nourishing your wife relationally. You must spend time with her. The particulars of what that looks like may vary from marriage to marriage, but the point is still the same. The Bible tells us that God created marriage to be a lifelong, covenantal companionship between one man and one woman, and instructs us to leave our fathers and/or mothers and cling (adhere or be glued) to our wives (Ephesians 5:31). Your wife, therefore, should not be vying against others—or other things–for some relational game time with you. She shouldn't feel like she is coming off the bench behind your parent(s), or your friends.

We are to nourish them physically. Kiss her. Hug her. Hold her hand. Stroke her hair...I mean, back (Some women are particular about their hair and don't want you running your fingers through it, especially when they have recently been to the beauty salon.). The point is to make sure we are showing them affection according to their preferences. There is more to be said about this, but we'll wait until chapter five.

Allow me to briefly hit on a related touchy aspect. Do you punch, kick, slap, cut, strangle, or shoot yourself? Then don't physically abuse your wife. And even if, for some unfortunate reason, you are into self-mutilation, that still doesn't give you the right to do so to your wife. To perpetrate violence against her is to fail to fulfill this God-given command to nourish our wives physically and is downright wicked, sinful, and evil. God righteously hates those who love violence (Psalm 11:5; Proverbs 6:17b, 18a). I know you would say that you don't *love* violence. As a genuine Christian man, you shouldn't. But it doesn't matter if you did it once or have a pattern of domestic abuse; being violent towards your wife is antithetical to what it means to be a man of God. I am going to step off of one of my soapboxes now, but before I do let me challenge you: if you are abusing your wife, stop it! Repent, and go get some help from a Christian counselor. If you are that upset to the point where you feel like attacking her, then you need to remove yourself from the vicinity. Go to the gym, the basketball court, or the golf course and relieve your aggression. Better yet, take it to Jesus in prayer. He has a way of calming you down and giving you what you need to handle your marital situation in a healthy, helpful, God-glorifying manner.

Do you starve yourself? Then your wife shouldn't be starving for your attention, time, and devotion. When you were a young boy, did you intentionally try and stop yourself from getting taller or stronger? No, right? Then you shouldn't seek to prevent your wife from blossoming—i.e., achieving God-inspired goals and accomplishments, like obtaining a degree, serving the church, going on a short-term mission trip, changing careers, launching a business, non-profit, or ministry, etc.—especially when her priorities are in alignment with God's (Titus 2:4-5). Again, if we are loving our wives like Christ loved the church, they will flourish and not flounder under our leadership.

We Cherish Them

The proper definition of the Greek verb-form of cherish means to warm. In the context of Ephesians 5:25ff, it means to cherish our wives with tender love, to demonstrate loving affection towards them. We are to adore them and they should know and feel it. Too many of us as husbands have grown cold towards our wives. We give icy looks. We speak blistering words. We exemplify shivering selfishness. We act in very cold-hearted ways. If we continue to display this type of behavior towards our wives, our marriages will suffer and possibly die from relational hypothermia. But, it shouldn't be this way, for Paul commands us not to be harsh with our wives (Colossians 3:19). Here are a few ways to turn the thermostat up in your marriage.

We ought to cherish our wives with our thoughts. I wanted to start with this one because some of us men, if we are honest, feel that as long as we don't run out on our wives literally we should get a pass if we on occasion happen to run out on them mentally. This is not permissible for those of us who claim the name of Jesus. Lest we forget, Jesus expects us to guard our eyes and hearts against lust, because according to him, if we lust after other women, we have already committed adultery in our hearts (Matthew 5:27-28). What this translates to is that pornography, strip clubs, and the like are all out of bounds for us. When I teach this, almost inevitably some guy will retort, "Well, there is nothing wrong with me simply looking at an attractive woman. I am just admiring God's beautiful creation." Granted, all looking is not sinful. However, you need to be very careful because looking could lead to you lingering, which will eventually end in you lusting. If you keep consuming "eye candy," it will at some point cause spiritual decay and will rot out your marriage. But cherishing our wives with our thoughts extends to more than just the physical; it includes the emotional and relational. They are the only women whose company we should long for and with whom we share all our heart.

We ought to cherish our wives with our words. That adage, "sticks and stones may break my bones, but words will never hurt me," simply is not true. Words are like knives, they can be of benefit or cause great damage to people; it's all a matter of how you use them. The content of your speech can either tear down or build up your wife. Paul, in Ephesians 4:29, admonishes us to do the latter. Speak words of affirmation to your wife. And when advice or evaluation is requested or correction is needed, make sure it is constructive and not destructive. Your words have weight. So don't crush your wife with them. Build her up instead.

We ought to cherish our wives with our actions. Actions speak louder than words. This is true particularly when we say one thing but do another. What are our actions saying to our wives? Do they say, "I cherish you" or "I don't really care that much about you"? My dad was not a perfect husband (none of us are), but there was no doubt in mind that my father cherished my mother. He set a good example for me and my brothers on how we were to treat our wives. I was certain he held my mother in high esteem not simply because he gave her gifts on her birthday and on Mother's Day, but because of how he treated her day in and day out. He would periodically call my mom throughout the day just to check on her to see how she was doing. He routinely took her out for a few hours for a night on the town. After a hard day's work, he made sure to engage her at some point during the evening. After decades of being together, he'd fill up the car with gas and take her on a getaway, as he had done numerous times before. And the list goes on and on. You may not do everything with your wife, the way my dad did with his, but it ought to be undeniable to her—and to onlookers—that you absolutely adore her, even in her un-adorable moments.

Chapter 2

Understanding Submission

If there is one verse that guys have memorized, it is Ephesians 5:22, "Wives, submit to your own husbands, as to the Lord." Yet many of us have misconceptions about submission and thus misapply it in the context of our marriages. Our view of submission almost, at times, seems to closely resemble the "She's Your Queen To Be" scene from the 1988 classic movie *Coming to America* more than it does the Bible. Prince Akeem (played by Eddie Murphy), heir to the throne of Zamunda, is introduced to his arranged-bride-to-be, Imani Izzi (played by Vanessa Bell Calloway). Prince Akeem kindly leans over to Imani and asks to speak to her in private. He escorts her into a private chamber to have a conversation.

Prince Akeem: "So…"

Imani Izzi: "Ever since I was born, I've been trained to serve you."

Prince Akeem: "Yes, I know this. But I would like to know about you. What do you like to do?"

Imani Izzi: "Whatever you like."

Prince Akeem: "What kind of music do you like?"

Imani Izzi: "Whatever kind of music you like."

Prince Akeem: "Look, I know what I like. And I know you know what I like because you are trained to know what I like, but I would like to know what you like. For instance, do you have a favorite food?"

Imani Izzi: "Yes."

Prince Akeem: "Good! What is your favorite food?"

Imani Izzi: "Whatever food you like."

Prince Akeem: "Are you saying that no matter what I tell you to do you will do?"

Imani Izzi: "Yes, your highness."

Prince Akeem: "Anything I say you'll do?"

Imani Izzi: "Yes, your highness."

Prince Akeem: "Bark like a dog."

And then the awkward hilarity commences. She complies and barks like a dog, and according to Prince Akeem's other requests, even hops on one leg and makes a noise like an orangutan. We all know that is Hollywood, but in reality there are unfortunately men who want, expect, and even demand robotic submission from their wives. Don't express your opinion, no matter how respectful the tone and approach, unless it is solicited. Agree with everything we do. And definitely don't lovingly hold us accountable. Just do as we say and all will be well. This is submission, some think. It might be that way in a movie, but not in real life and especially not according to God's script.

So my aim in this chapter is simply to help us as husbands to understand biblical submission. Sometimes the best way to grasp a concept is to talk about what it is *not*. But before we go there, I want to bring to the surface two common beliefs many men in general, and husbands in particular, hold to as it relates to submission, and examine them under the microscope of God's word to see if they are true.

SUBMISSION IS FOR WOMEN

Is submission solely relegated to our female counterparts? In other words, is submission for women only? The answer is no. If you take a cursory read through the New Testament letters, you will discover that submission is a virtue of the Christian life and, therefore, applicable to all believers, no matter your gender.

All Christians Submit to Jesus. Interestingly enough, in the very same passage of the verse that was just referenced at the outset of this chapter, Paul uses this idea of the church, or all Christians, submitting to Jesus as an example of how wives should submit to their husbands. He writes, "Now as the church submits to Christ..." (Ephesians 5:24a). Submission is a way of life that is to be continually exhibited by all Christ-followers, men and women alike.

All Christians Submit to their Parents. Paul commands us as children to obey our parents in the Lord (Ephesians 6:1; also cf. Colossians 3:20), whether we were raised by a father and mother, a single mom or dad, grandparents or some other relative, or foster parents. And even though we are married and living in our own place, this command is still valid. The dynamics of it look different now, of course. So, although we are not directly under their authority anymore, when we go home, for example, to Mom's and/or Dad's place, it is their house, their rules.

All Christians Submit to the Elders/Pastors of their Local Church. When we join in covenant membership with a local church, we come under the pastoral leadership, care, and preaching and teaching of those elders/pastors. The writer of Hebrews instructs all believers to "obey your leaders and submit to them, for they are keeping watch over your souls, as those who will have to give an account. Let them do this with joy and not with groaning, for that would be of no advantage to you." (Hebrews 13:17)

All Christians Submit to the Governing Authorities. Paul, under the inspiration of the Holy Spirit, directs all of us Christ-followers in Romans 13:1ff to individually submit ourselves to the governing authorities. If there ever was a morally loose and corrupt, and religiously idolatrous, pluralistic and syncretistic government, it was the Roman Empire. And yet Paul commands the believers in that sociopolitical context to submit to the authorities. So it is for us in America and for our other brothers and sisters in Christ in other countries around the world as well. Should Christians be involved in politics to help shape and steer legislation according to God's word? Absolutely. Is there a time for civil disobedience? I am sure there is, especially those believers who find themselves in closed countries (i.e., where the government is explicitly hostile towards Christianity). But, overall, we are to submit to, honor, and respect our governing officials and authorities, from the President to the police officer. Regardless of how democratic a government is, it will never be perfect because flawed, sinful, and even lost human beings are involved. But that does not circumvent our obedience to the Lord Jesus in submitting to the authorities he has established and sanctioned, as long as they are appropriately executing their authority according to, and informed by, God's word.

WOMEN SHOULD BE MADE TO SUBMIT

Quite frankly, this is just absurd. Excuse me for being passionate and straightforward when it comes to this point. But this idea of husbands feeling justified in their passive or aggressive attempts to bring their wives in subjection to them is patently unbiblical. I would even go so far as to say that if we seek to do such a thing we are sinning against God and our wives and need to repent. On what basis can I make such an indictment? Fair question. And I don't think it will be difficult to substantiate. There is a real simple explanation. Let's go back and read Ephesians 5:22, 24: "Wives, submit to your own husbands, as to the Lord....Now as the church submits to Christ, so also wives should submit in everything to their husbands." Who does Paul address in these verses? Wives. To whom is the command directed? Wives. So who is responsible for carrying out this divine instruction? You guessed it...wives. Submission in marriage is the sacred responsibility of our wives to fulfill out of reverence for the Lord Jesus. It is up to them to see to it that they respect us (Ephesians 5:33). Did it say anywhere in those two verses about husbands forcing this upon their wives? No. Absolutely not. God will always call a foul on us when we seek to force them into submission. Any attempt to manipulate or threaten our wives into submitting to our leadership is an offense against them and God and an insidious abuse of our headship as husbands.

What Submission is Not

Before we continue on, let's define what submission is. The word means to fall in line or arrange under. It was often used in a military context to speak of a soldier who was to be under the authority of a higher ranking officer. In my years of counseling couples, I've come to understand that sometimes definition gets lost in application because of misinterpretation. What I mean is, a word can be defined clearly, but we can still make erroneous inferences, as is the case with submission. So, I want to highlight and challenge a few of the most common, yet unbiblical implications concerning this word, which I pray translates into you having a better understanding of what submission is in the context of your marriage.

Submission doesn't mean your wife is inferior to you. More than likely you are familiar with the creation account recorded in Genesis chapter one. According to verse twenty-seven, God created humanity in his own image, both male and female. What this implies is that both men and women are completely equal in essence. We are inherently no greater in being or value than women, and they are inherently no lesser than us. They are not our property. They are not our slaves. Like us, they have been fearfully and wonderfully made by God (Psalm 139:14; also see Psalm 8:5) and should be respected as such.

As I trekked through Ephesians chapter five during one of my counseling sessions with this engaged couple, we landed on verse twenty-four. As I read the "b" clause of the verse–which says, "so also wives should submit in everything to their husbands."—I added a caveat, saying, "as long as their husbands are not blatantly leading them into sin, of course." To which the zealous young man, in essence, replied, "I disagree with you on that Pastor Johnson. That's not what that verse says. If it says everything, it means everything. So my wife is supposed to submit to me even if I ask her to do something sinful. Obviously no godly man would ever do that, but I am just saying, if that were the case, she should do it and know that God is not going to hold her accountable because she was obeying what God told her to do which is to submit to me." While taken aback by his passionate argument, the Lord allowed me to compose myself and patiently explain to him why I gave that qualification. To be honest though, I couldn't believe what I heard. This was a classic case of a well-meaning brother focusing on one verse without seeing it in light of the rest of Scripture (of which I have been guilty of at times myself). Thankfully he changed his position after I showed him, through Scripture, how *submission is not absolute*[5]; meaning, if our desires and decisions—those that involve the participation of our spouses–are contrary to the clear directives of Scripture, our wives are not obligated by God to comply. At that point, the Lord's authority overrules ours. So we can't get mad at our wives, neither should we seek to guilt them into submission, when they, in light of our departure from leading according to the explicit commands of God, respectfully decline to oblige us in those moments. We should repent of our hypocrisy rather than try and force it upon our wives by perversely appealing to our headship over them. To do the latter is nothing short of spiritual and relational abuse, which doesn't reflect the sacrificial servant leadership of Jesus.

Submission doesn't mean your wife is not allowed to weigh in, offer suggestions, or share her thoughts on decisions that will affect the family. After explaining this very point to another dear brother in the Lord, he disagreed with me, stating that listening to our wives can get us in trouble, just like it did Adam (referring to Genesis 3:17, "And to Adam he said, 'Because you have listened to the voice of your wife and have eaten of the tree of which I commanded you, 'You shall not eat of it,' cursed is the ground…'"); therefore, as husbands, we need not ever look to our wives for input. We should just pray and then do what God puts on our hearts. And I agreed with the brother…to an extent. It is true that Adam got himself in hot water with God when he listened to his wife and disobeyed him. And, yes, we should not

---

[5] For life examples of this point, see Exodus 1:15-17 and Daniel chapters 3 and 6. Although these two historical accounts are not dealing with marriage, they both have to do with the relationship between those in and under authority, and verify the point of submission to human leaders as not being absolute. All human leaders have the tendency to disobey God and lead others astray from the clear commands of God. And if that ever is the case with our leadership, our wives have a responsibility to God not to submit to us in those moments.

listen to our wives–or anyone for that matter—when their advice is contrary to the commands of God in Scripture. But, we should not go so far as to believe that because of Eve's actions we as husbands should, in our minds and at all times, mute our wives' voices. And neither should we be so quick to interpret our wives offering their opinion as them stepping out of line and not being submissive. The Bible considers seeking counsel as wise, which generally results in safety and success (Proverbs 11:14; 15:22). Surely God can use our wives as counselors to help guide us in the direction he wants us to go, don't you think? There are times, as attested in the Bible, when God might speak to our wives—or even through them without their knowledge–in relationship to some aspect of our lives as a family (Judges 13), or use them to prevent us from encountering or connecting with people who mean us no good (1 Samuel 19:11-17), or from suffering the consequences of our own foolish actions (1 Samuel 25:2-35), and to assist us in our deliberations and decisions (Matthew 27:15-19). A prudent wife is of the Lord (Proverbs 19:14). It would behoove us to at least prayerfully take into consideration the wisdom, perspective, and knowledge they bring to the table.

Being submissive doesn't mean your wife is not able to occupy leadership positions in corporate America, the non-profit sector, or even in the church *(with the exception of being an Elder or Deacon[6]—cf. 1 Timothy 3; Titus 1:6ff).* I have met guys who erroneously believe that all women (single and married) are to be submissive to all men in all of life. "At no time and under no circumstances should women have authority over men," they say. But does that square with Scripture? I believe it does not. There are only two arenas of life in which women are to submit to men and not seek to take the leadership role: 1. the home, and 2. the church. Anything and everything outside

---

[6] The spirit behind this point is not meant to stir up controversy among, or to offend, brothers and sisters in the Lord who interpret these passages differently.

of that is fair game. *"Well, married women's place should be at the house anyway. They shouldn't be working outside the home at all."* I don't altogether agree with this sentiment. While speaking to older Christian women and the role they are to play in the lives of younger Christian women, Paul makes mention of the latter being trained "to love their husbands and children, to be self-controlled, pure, working at home..." (Titus 2:5). Some have understood the last phrase in the quoted verse to mean that married women must be stay-at-home wives and moms. This is definitely a legitimate, worthy, and noble application of this verse for married women who have children, but I don't believe it is the one ruling interpretation of it. As I understand it, Paul is not saying that all young married women are required to be homebound, but rather homeward-focused. That is to say, married women, especially younger ones, should have their marriage, children (if they have any), and household affairs as the top priorities in their lives. So if your wife desires to stay at home and it is something you two prayerfully agree on and are able to make happen, then by all means go for it. If she desires to work outside the home while maintaining the biblical priorities of marriage and motherhood, don't interpret that as being out of line with Scripture. The Bible describes a virtuous wife as one who "looks well to the ways of her household and does not eat the bread of idleness" (Proverbs 31:26) and "makes linen garments and sells them; she delivers sashes to the merchants" (Proverbs 31:24); and mentions women–some of whom were wives–who held positions, conducted business, or worked to some degree outside the home (e.g., Deborah: Judges 4:4-5; Lydia: Acts 16:14).

MUTUAL OR MARITAL SUBMISSION: WHICH ONE IS IT?

Let me begin this section by unequivocally stating that I absolutely believe Scripture speaks of husbands being the head of their wives (and instructs wives to submit to their own husbands). And I understand that headship to refer to authority and leadership, and is to be carried out in a manner that honors and reflects Christ—sacrificially and selflessly. And yet, in my study of Scripture, I have also come to discover another reality that is equally true in marriage and one that, in my estimation, doesn't take away from or nullify biblical, Gospel-centered headship. It is based on Ephesians chapter five verse twenty-one, where Paul writes, "submitting to one another out of reverence for Christ." It is not a new discovery, and has been a point of theological debate among Christian scholars, pastors, preachers, and teachers for years. So allow me to state my conviction first, and then I'll explain why I humbly hold this position. I believe when we apply this verse in the context of marriage between two Christians, we as husbands may at times and in certain cases need to submit ourselves to our wives. And doing so, I would argue, is not an abdication but rather an expression of humble leadership. Here are my reasons:

- When you examine verses 18 through 21 of Ephesians 5, you will discover there is a list of five participles that follow the verb "be filled": addressing, singing and making melody, giving thanks, and submitting. Submitting to one another, then, is a result of being filled with the Spirit, which is commanded and should be characteristic of all Christians, regardless of our gender, marital, or social status.

- Although verse 22 takes on the participle of verse 21, the general reality of Spirit-filled believers submitting to one another is still in effect, even though there is a specific application directed towards wives to their husbands.

And so when we synthesize this information, we can see how it is possible, as husbands, to be in authority, maintain that position and yet at times and in certain situations submit to our wives who are under our authority. If you have ever flown on a commercial flight, you know that there are two people who occupy the cockpit: the pilot and co-pilot. There is no doubt that the pilot-in-command has authority to fly the plane and is ultimately responsible for ensuring it arrives safely to its destination. The co-pilot also has a part to play in the safe travel of the commercial airliner and is there to assist the pilot. The co-pilot is under the authority of the pilot. But, it is also true that as pilots both, the pilot and the co-pilot, are required to submit to the same authority, abiding by the rules and regulations of the Federal Aviation Administration (FAA); and are to support and hold each other accountable to that one and same standard. They have different roles, but at the end of the day they are both pilots and are, therefore, expected to adhere to FAA standards no matter what seat they occupy in the cockpit. So, if the pilot fails or forgets to abide by the standard procedures, the co-pilot has a responsibility to encourage, admonish, or help the pilot to comply. And the pilot, knowing he is in the wrong or recognizing his mishap, should yield or submit to the co-pilot in that instance. Why? Because they are both under the same greater authority. As it is in aviation, so it is in marriage. As husband, you are the head in your marriage (and family) and ultimately responsible for its welfare. Your wife is to willingly place herself under your loving authority and assist you in whatever way to help establish and maintain a family unit that honors Jesus. At the same time, you both are Christians—that is, if you two have trusted the Lord Jesus for salvation–and are subject to the one and same standard and authority: the Lord Jesus and his Bible; and are called to encourage and hold each other accountable to live accordingly.

There are three categories in which we as husbands should yield to our wives. First, we should yield to their biblical correction. Yes, we are Christ-like, godly men, but that doesn't mean we are perfect. We still have our moments when we struggle with our sinful flesh, Satan, and the world. And so, when our wives lovingly remind us of what the Scripture says and encourage us to line up with it, we ought not to dismiss them or "put them in their place" for not "staying in their lane" but rather submit ourselves to their loving act of pointing us back to God's word.

Second, we need to yield to their caring admonishments. Having your wife tell you in light of the Scripture that you are in the wrong is not the most pleasant feeling in the world. It's like a kidney punch, but to your ego. Unfortunately, too many times we become defensive and seek to shift rather than shoulder the blame. Or, we will attempt to shine the spotlight on our wives and off of ourselves by trying to point out their imperfections when we all know the issue on the table has nothing to do with them. We need to be humble, receive the rebuke, and repent.

Third, we yield to their insightful advice. What I am talking about is respecting your wife's opinions and suggestions enough to listen and prayerfully give them consideration when it concerns matters that are not specifically addressed in the Bible (matters like, whether or not you should resign or accept a job offer, move to another state, or make a major purchase.). I have come to find out in many cases God the Holy Spirit has used my wife's advice to guide me in the direction he wanted me to go or to confirm a decision he wanted me to make. Generally speaking, if there is safety in an abundance of [godly] counselors (Proverbs 11:14), don't you think a wife who submits herself to Jesus and you would be among that number; and that it would be wise to get her take on issues you are facing?

The answer to the question is: it is both marital and mutual submission, not either/or. I know it seems contradictory, but there are many things about the Christian faith that are seemingly paradoxical in nature and yet we still embrace them, do we not? The Trinity: three co-eternal, co-equal persons and one God. Jesus: fully God and fully man. The Bible: humanly written and divinely inspired. The Kingdom of God: already and not yet. Christians: saints and sinners. So, in marriage, she submits to you because you are the head, and yet at the same time as Christians you submit to one another as needed. Don't worry, you are still the man; just be a humble man who respects, appreciates, and submits to the help that God gives you through your helpmate, recognizing that as a maturing Christian she too bows in reverent obedience to the Lord Jesus, has been indwelt and gifted by the same Holy Spirit, and has been graced by God with skills, intelligence, wisdom, and experience to, in some measure, positively contribute to your life and leadership.

Chapter 3

Let's Talk: Communicating With Your Wife

I remember seeing a cartoon on a t-shirt featuring an elderly married couple in their living room. The wife was standing over her husband who was lounging in a recliner chair, reading a paper. The caption read: "Communication is a critical part of a successful marriage, so keep your pie-hole shut and listen." Although it was meant to be tongue-in-cheek, ironically, that is for the most part the reality many couples experience and endure in their marriages. Communication is virtually a one-way street. I talk, you listen; especially when there is conflict. Talking with your spouse, at times, can be like driving through a dead spot while talking on your cell phone: a lot of interference, distortion, and dropped calls. We all have those moments.

The good news is we can get better at communicating with our wives and it begins with understanding the basic components of communication:

1. Speaking: what we say, or don't say, and how we say it.
2. Listening: what we hear.
3. Perceiving: what we think about what was said.

Early on in my marriage (and even now at times), I struggled with all three of these aspects with my wife. If it was not something I said, it was my poor listening skills. If it was not my poor listening skills, it was my tendency to misinterpret what she said. Thank God I have improved since then, and you can too. By the way, even if you have been married for three decades, there are principles from this chapter you still ought to be applying to your relationship. Communication is an ongoing endeavor in marriage. We must work at it daily to ensure we are effectively communicating with our wives. We can never shift into neutral, coast, and take our hands off the wheel of communication; if we do, relational wreckage is inevitable. In the first section of this chapter we will look at what Scripture has to say about communication and then in the second section I will share with you some lessons I've learned—particularly in times of conflict–from my own experience as well as some advice I've given to others over the years.

THE WORD ON WORDS

Speaking of relational wreckage, one of the main reasons why we end up having marital fender benders is due to us hitting the gas too quickly when it comes to speaking. We rush to get our point across, rather than pausing to listen first. We have to learn how to pump the brakes on our mouths. James tells us we should be quick to hear [the word] and **slow to speak** (James 1:19-20, emphasis mine). Learning to not be so quick to speak will do wonders in improving your communication with your wife.

Take more pleasure in understanding your wife than expressing your opinion (Proverbs 18:2). The truth is we can be quite selfish, desiring only to get stuff off of our chest and not care as much about hearing what our spouses have to say. This is especially true when we find ourselves in the midst of conflict. Would it have a healthy impact on you and your marriage if you consistently sought to view listening to, and seeking to understand, your wife as a delight, rather than a duty or drudgery? It would definitely help us to be more patient and not quickly become so angry and frustrated with our spouses when speaking with them. Our wives want to be heard and understood by us; and we should do so readily. Let's not simply tolerate them. They *can* tell the difference.

I never knew working with my father during the summer as a little boy would teach me valuable lessons that would be applicable to my marriage years later. I remember a couple of instances when my father asked me to go to his truck to retrieve some tools he needed to work on an air conditioner or refrigerator unit. My father said to me once, while kneeling down checking his Freon gauges, "Son, I need you to go to the truck and get me…" I eagerly jumped in to finish my dad's sentence as I turned to walk to his vehicle, "…a flathead and a crescent wrench." I just knew what he needed for the job, or so I thought. My father stopped me and responded, "EJ. I know you are trying to be helpful, but you need to learn how to listen before you respond. Don't be so much in a rush that you don't listen completely to what I am asking for. Okay? Now, yes, I need the flathead and crescent wrench, but I also need you to bring me the needle-nose and slip joint pliers, and a Philips screwdriver." Little did I know my dad taught me that day a principle from the book of Proverbs: Listen fully so you don't speak prematurely (Proverbs 18:13). Not doing so is foolish and embarrassing. How many of us as husbands have spoken too soon and had to turn around and apologize for jumping to conclusions, all because we didn't take time to hear our wives out completely?

Work to speak softly and sensitively with your wife when you are in the middle of conflict (Proverbs 15:1). When I say softly, I am referring to the way in which you talk to your wife. The tone of your voice can either further inflame a heated situation between you and your wife or help cool it down. Speaking loudly or screaming at your spouse is not going to get you anywhere with her or in your marriage. If you do shout and holler, one of two things will happen: she will match your blazing tone of voice with her own, or she will shut down on you. And, in some circumstances, both could be the result. Whatever the case may be, it is not going to go well for your relationship. The proverb not only has in view tone of voice, but also content of speech: "...but a harsh word stirs up anger." What you say matters. To speak a harsh word doesn't just involve profanity. You can speak harshly to your wife and not use one curse word. Intentionally and maliciously pushing her buttons to get back at her out of anger goes against the prescribed wisdom of Scripture. It's wrong, and will not defuse the situation. It will only make it worse. So, as much as possible, speak with your wife in a gentle and considerate manner.

"Whatever comes to mind, I don't evaluate it, weigh it, or give it some thought; I just say it and let the chips fall where they may," is the prevailing modus operandi of too many of us when it comes to speaking with our wives. That is a recipe for disaster. Saying whatever comes to mind may bring you relief, but it will cause agony in your marriage. It is an unwise approach to communication because the Scripture counsels us to think before we speak (Proverbs 15:28a). When we haphazardly spew out words, we mimic the way of the wicked; because the righteous— those who have a relationship with God in Christ and live their lives according to his statutes—seek to give thought before they talk. Guarding our mouths not only preserves our lives but our marriages as well (Proverbs 13:3).

Trade in rotten talk for grace talk. Rotten talk does nothing to produce health in your marriage. Abusive, controlling, aggressive or passive-aggressive, patronizing, insensitive, arrogant, and selfish speech are all spoiled, and will only cause your relationship to be weak and sickly. If rotten talk is self-centered, then grace talk is the opposite; it is others-centered, looking out for the interests of another. Grace talk is speech that builds up, not tears down. When we embrace grace talk, we employ speech that works for our wives' good, even though they may at times treat us bad. Grace talk fits the occasion (Ephesians 4:29). For example, grace talk says to us, husbands: if your wife is hurting, console her. If she is discouraged, encourage her. If she achieves something, congratulate her. If she fails or is on the verge of giving up, coach her (i.e., reassure her and patiently and wisely challenge her). If she sins against you, yes, honestly acknowledge how her actions hurt you, but also sincerely tell her that you forgive her. If you make a bad decision or sin against her, don't try to duck responsibility or seek to shift the blame when she approaches you about it; humbly apologize or ask for forgiveness.

Have you ever heard that old saying, "Your mouth is going to get you in a lot of trouble"? Isn't that true? Our marriages suffer, in part, because we just don't know when to shut up. This is a temptation for many husbands, like myself, who are talkers. You don't have to make us tell you what is on our minds because we will let you know. But there is a danger in that as Proverbs 10:19a tells us, "When words are many, transgression is not lacking..." Have you ever been in a situation where you kept talking to your wife (or someone else) and at some point you said something you wish you could take back? We have to remind ourselves of the second part of Proverbs 10:19, "but whoever restrains his lips is prudent." But this is not just a word for husbands who talk a lot;

it is also for those who are characterized as men of few words. Although you might not generally be the talkative type, you too have the propensity, in certain situations, to say too much. Regardless of the type of husbands we are–talkative or the quiet type–we need to keep a leash on our tongues, otherwise we will run off at the mouth and find ourselves in deep trouble.

Cherish your wife with your words (Ephesians 5:29b). I touched on this briefly at the end of chapter one, but allow me to elaborate. The Bible speaks to the influential nature of the tongue. James compares it to fire when he writes, "How great a forest is set ablaze by such a small fire!" (James 3:5b) Our tongues should not be used to burn up our wives' emotions, confidence, and worth. We instead should adore them. Tell her that you are so grateful that she is a woman who fears the Lord Jesus. Let her know that you appreciate her being a woman of character, whose inner beauty is just as attractive to you as her physical beauty. Be sure she knows that you value her mind: her intelligence, wisdom, and insight. We should make it our goal to warm—not scorch–our wives with our words. When was the last time you said "Thank you" to your wife? I'm not just talking about when she does something special for your birthday, or some other special occasion. I'm also referring to the day-to-day matters she takes care of; like, cleaning the house, being a mother to your child or children, cooking, and all the rest. Yes, these are responsibilities of marriage and parenting, but that doesn't mean we should take them for granted. "I don't and she knows that," you say. I am sure you are right. But it won't hurt to verbally acknowledge and appreciate her for doing what she does. Just like their words mean something to us, our words mean something to them.

FIGHTING FAIR

My wife and I dated for eight years and have been married for twelve. In 20 years of us being together we have had our share of verbal fights. With some of those melees, we walked away bruised and bloody. It wasn't pretty at all. There were some illegal punches thrown: low blows and hammer fists to the back of the head. But in spite of our immature, fleshly-brawling ways God was gracious and patient with us amateur fighters and taught us how to fight fair; to fight for our marriage and not against it. And so I would like to share some of those fight tips with you in hopes that they will help you in your relationship. This list is by no means exhaustive, but it covers a lot of ground and is applicable to a multitude of scenarios. Obviously marriage is not monolithic. Although I have sought to keep my advice general, at the end of the day my marriage is the laboratory in which these ideas were tested and tried. Take what is applicable to your marriage and leave the rest. What mostly follows are the implications of the Scriptures that were referenced in the previous section of this chapter.

Invite God into your conflict. Before you attempt to address that sensitive subject, pray with each other. Yes, pray to God together. When you honestly and humbly seek God in prayer, he has a way of guarding your hearts from becoming stubbornly defensive, retaliatory and acting out in sinful anger (Ephesians 4:26, cf., James 1:19-20). Often through prayer, God helps to soften your hearts towards each other. You are more prone to listen to one another. You approach each other as friends who are seeking to resolve a dilemma instead of as enemies who are looking to defeat one another. But let's keep it real. There may be times in which you don't feel like praying with her. Well, in those moments, you at least individually need to make sure you pray before you seek to process the problem. The point is, just don't go into conflict alone. Ask God to referee. You will be amazed at how he will intervene.

I remember one time after speaking with my wife concerning some matters she went cold on me. I felt the chill in the air, so I asked if something was bothering her. Of course she said yes, but I had no idea what it was or why. Unbeknownst to me, we had just entered the ring. After talking things over and getting to the root of the problem, I had learned another valuable lesson on fighting fair: Identify the issue. Here are a couple of simple pointers on how to do this:

Examine yourself.

- Did you do or not do something to cause or contribute to this problem?
- Did you possibly take something your wife said or did the wrong way?
- Did you assume or jump to a conclusion?

Ask questions of your wife.

I know you think you know your wife like the back of your hand and can normally tell what is going on with her, but you are not all-knowing. Jesus is the only one who knows perfectly what is going on in our hearts and minds without having to inquire (Luke 6:8, John 2:24-25). We, on the other hand, have to ask questions. Keep these three questions handy when you encounter unexpected relational turbulence:

- Why are you upset?
- What did I say or do (or not say or do) that bothered you?
- Is there something on your mind that we need to talk about?

Seek not to respond when you are emotional. No that's not a typo. Contrary to popular belief, we, as men, can become emotional too. We may not want to admit it, but the truth is the truth. Frustration, anger, and apathy are all intertwined with our feelings. We may display or handle our emotions differently than our wives, but the fact remains: we emote just like everyone else. So, before you blow up, call a timeout to calm down, pray, and think.

Acknowledge and articulate when you are becoming defensive or if something bothered or hurt you. Acting like nothing is wrong or downplaying it is neither healthy nor helpful for you or your marriage. It is not unmanly for you to be honest about how you feel. If Jesus was willing to be vulnerable in the Garden of Gethsemane with his disciples, and in prayer to the Father concerning drinking the cup of God's wrath against our sin on our behalf (Matthew 26:36ff), surely we can be vulnerable with our wives in such comparatively smaller, less significant matters.

Learn to take what your wife says at face value. Constantly reading into what she says or doesn't say will only lead to frustration and confusion. You can overanalyze your marriage into conflict. Don't presume that you know something else is going on that she is just not telling you about. You may have even hit the nail on the head in the past in terms of knowing your wife wasn't letting you in to all that was going on with her, but it doesn't mean you will be right all the time. It is better for you to ask questions than to make assumptions.

Don't formulate rebuttals in your mind while your wife is talking in an effort to win an argument or to simply prove her wrong. Rather seek to understand your wife's perspective and feelings, so that you can respond appropriately and work towards a mutual understanding of the issue at hand.

If we are honest, some of us (and maybe all of us at times) have an aversion to conflict, at least when it comes to our ladies. We don't like to get into it with them. We are lovers, not fighters. But we ought not to get into the habit of running from conflict. Burying our heads in the sand is not going to make our relationships better. All conflict is not unhealthy. Much of it will help strengthen our marriages, if we handle it the right way. Marital conflict is like weightlifting. The resistance and pressure are designed to build your muscles, but in order for you to get the maximum benefit you must first commit to the apparatus—i.e., assume the appropriate position. You simply walking around the gym is not going to do you any good. You have to decide to engage. Once you do that and the weight is applied, you need to keep good form. If you don't apply the right form, you can injure yourself. So it is with the conflict we encounter in our marriages. No matter how uncomfortable, challenging, and tense the conflict is, you need to decide that you are going to lean into and work your way through it as husband and wife, all the while keeping the right form of prayer, humility, grace, patience, gentleness, and kindness, so that you don't cause injury to your marriage but rather growth, strength, and health.

You should strive to speak to her respectfully, even if she may not reciprocate in kind. This doesn't mean you don't address issues you have with her, but that you seek to do so with words that won't devalue her as a person. "Well it's almost like she doesn't hear me unless I spazz out on her." I hear you, but no matter the seeming results which might be achieved through such an approach, that is not how God desires for us to speak to our wives. Instead of trying to get her to listen to you through your own fleshly means, pray for God to open up her heart to hear you as you seek to communicate honestly, yet respectfully, to her. He is way more powerful than you and is able to break through your wife's impenetrable attitude and perspective. Also know that *not* speaking to your wife out of malicious intent to hurt her is just as counterproductive as the harmful words you are tempted to say to her in a moment of conflict.

Work not to speak in absolutes: "You always..." or "You never..." Instead, say, "You have a habit of doing something," or "You don't do this all the time, but here recently..."

Own your failure without referring to hers—whether past or present. In our early days I was notorious for doing this with Tiffany. She would point out something I did and I would immediately become defensive or feel like she wasn't showing me the same grace I knew I showed her, and so I brought up her sins or mistakes against me. In my mind all I was seeking to do was to get her to show a brother a little mercy. But to her I was deflecting, playing the victim card, and just flat out being selfish by turning a moment about what I did to her into what she was apparently now doing to me. That used to infuriate her, and rightly so. In those instances when you legitimately feel your wife is beating you up when you fail as a man, you need to first accept responsibility for your actions and then, after some time has elapsed, speak with her about how you felt in that moment.

If you are a need-space-to-process guy, don't let a lot of time go by before you talk to your wife. Additionally, it would be helpful to give her a general time frame as to when you will be ready to talk. Don't leave her in limbo. Conversely, if you are a deal-with-it-right-now guy and your wife is a need-space-to-process woman, then give her time. Don't try to force her to talk. It is better to bear momentary tension to give her the time she needs to process than to incite a major blowup because you pressed her to talk.

Sometimes in a marriage you can reach an impasse, where you two are just not able to reach a resolution on your own. Some issues can be so volatile or complex that you will need someone to serve as a mediator. In those cases, go get some help. Go. Get. Some. Help. I can't tell you how many times wives have had to drag their husbands to counseling. Don't be that guy. It doesn't make you less of a man to seek the assistance of a Christian counselor. I know what some of you might be thinking, "It's not about me feeling less of a man. I just think what happens in our house should stay in our house. I don't want someone else in our business." I get that. But let me ask you, how is that working out for your marriage? Notice, I didn't say "How is that working out for *you?*" In your estimation everything is probably just fine; but what does your wife think? Exactly. It makes no sense for us to have longstanding, unresolved issues in our marriages all because we as husbands won't humble ourselves and seek out godly counsel from those who can help us unravel the tangled messes that our marriages occasionally find themselves in. By all means try to paddle your marriage raft out of the storm of conflict first. But, if you find yourselves capsized and not able to make it to the shore of reconciliation on your own, shoot off a flare. And when you see help coming, don't wave them off. Grab the lifeline and follow their biblical instruction and advice.

Chapter 4

A Charge to Keep I Have

A charge to keep I have,
A God to glorify,
A never dying soul to save,
And fit it for the sky.

To serve the present age,
My calling to fulfill:
O may it all my powers engage
To do my Master's will!

Arm me with jealous care,
As in Thy sight to live;
And O Thy servant, Lord, prepare
A strict account to give!

Help me to watch and pray,
And on Thyself rely,
Assured if I my Lord betray,
I shall forever die.

This classic hymn was written by Charles Wesley, the brother of John Wesley and co-founder of the Methodist denomination, who is noted to have written over 6,000 hymns. These words speak to the aim, and capture the heart cry, of every follower of Jesus. But it also can be specifically applied to those of us who have been called to the sacred duty of being husbands. Fundamentally, brothers, our marriages are not simply about making our ladies happy, fulfilling a desire for companionship or sexual intimacy, or for financial expediency; they are about glorifying God in Christ by keeping the charge he has given us regarding our wives. This God-given responsibility undoubtedly is multifaceted, but I believe first Peter chapter three perfectly sums up this charge with two overarching commands that we have been entrusted with and empowered through the Holy Spirit to carry out.

We are commanded to live with our wives in a caring manner

Peter, through the inspiration of God the Holy Spirit, commands us at the beginning of verse seven to live with our wives. Stop right there. I know we haven't finished Peter's thought yet, but let's pause just for a second to deal with what is implicit in these three words. This phrase "to live with" literally means to dwell together. As husbands, then, we are to associate and integrate our lives with our wives. This involves a lot of things, but let me sum it up in two categories. To live with, dwell together, and associate and integrate our lives with our wives involves:

Sharing what's on our hearts — And by this, I mean, revealing to your wife the moves you are contemplating; the growth, success, and achievements you are experiencing; and the battles you are fighting (e.g., fear, depression, loneliness, pride, worry, jealousy, frustration, anger, bitterness, etc.). If we are honest, many of us have a hard time opening up our hearts to our wives. This could be due to a myriad of reasons. Regardless of what those might be, we need to strive to be more transparent with them. They shouldn't have to feel like they are pulling teeth, trying to get us to talk about what's on our hearts. That's exhausting. If there is anyone you should be able to easily entrust your heart to, it ought to be your wife. Our wives should be our number one confidant.

Sharing what's in your possession — This essentially means what is yours is hers and what is hers is hers...I mean, what is hers is yours. That car, house or apartment, personal bank accounts, debt, pet, and so on belong to both of you. Generally speaking, nothing should be off limits to our wives. If something is off limits, it should be an item you both agreed on is exclusively yours or one that she has no use for or doesn't know, or care to know, how to operate and is therefore solely yours by default.

Let's continue Peter's thought. Due to the many Bible versions we have today, the "a" part of verse seven is rendered in slightly different ways depending on which one you read from, and can, therefore, lead to varying interpretations.

> *You husbands in the same way, live with your wives in an understanding way, as with someone weaker, since she is a woman... (1 Peter 3:7 NASB)*

> *Husbands, in the same way be considerate as you live with your wives, and treat them with respect as the weaker partner... (1 Peter 3:7 NIV)*

> *Likewise, husbands, live with your wives in an understanding way, showing honor to the woman as the weaker vessel... (1 Peter 3:7 ESV)*

> *In the same way, you husbands...treat your wife with understanding as you live together. She may be weaker than you are... (1 Peter 3:7 NLT)*

What does Peter mean here? Is he saying we should dwell together with our wives with the understanding that they are weaker vessels than us? If so, weaker how? Weak in intellect? Weak in physical strength? Weak in emotion? Weak in discipline? Obviously, this doesn't match what we see in life regarding women and men. You have some women who are definitely stronger than some men in all of the aforementioned areas. So that can't be it. What then is Peter saying? Well, I want to show you how it is literally given to us in the original Greek language because I think it will better help us grasp what Peter means.

"Husbands likewise, dwell together according to knowledge as a weaker vessel with the woman..."

To seek to deduce from this verse a universal list of ways in which all women are weaker than men is to completely miss the author's intended meaning. Peter does not call our wives weaker vessels for us to seek to determine how they are inferior in constitution than us men, but instead compares them to a weaker vessel to illustrate how we ought to care for them.

What then does he mean by a *weaker* vessel? We should understand this word to mean fragile, or better yet, delicate, like fine china. You don't treat fine china just any kind of way. It has its own special cabinet from the normal, every-day-use dinnerware. If your chinaware is dirty, you don't collectively stick it in some jet clean dishwasher—at least you are not supposed to. You wash and dry them individually with a hand towel. Similarly, Peter, in essence, is saying that is the type of treatment, special tender loving care our wives should receive from us.

We get that, but unfortunately too many of us limit our care for our wives largely to the materialistic and financial realm. But it entails much more than that. We already touched on the first three of these in chapter one, but I want to press into them a bit more. We should care for them:

Spiritually — This is the highest form of care that you can provide to your wife. Pray for and with her. You don't need to be preacher-eloquent in your prayers. Just pray. Your wife, if she is a believer, will appreciate this sincere gesture of spiritual care. Read, study, and/or discuss the Bible with her. Above all of that, we need to ensure that we are pursuing Jesus ourselves. You and I cannot lovingly lead our wives somewhere we are not. We must lead from out front. We should not be lackadaisical when it comes to our relationship with God. I get we are human and imperfect when it comes to staying disciplined in our spiritual devotion to prayer, Bible reading/studying, and the like. We all, at times, fall off the horse, so to speak. But we must continue striving, by the grace of God, to grow in Jesus. Only then will we be able—without blatant hypocrisy–to encourage our wives to do the same.

Relationally — The key word here is simple: engage. If you want to care for your wife relationally, show interest and get involved. "Show interest and get involved in what?" you ask. Great question. Answer: whatever she is into. If she comes home and wants to talk to you about her day, stop whatever you are doing—particularly those of us who are not good at multitasking–and listen. Turn off or away from the TV, computer, or video game and engage her in conversation. If she wants to go see a "chick flick" for date night, take one for the team and go–and don't complain, go to the bathroom or concession stand throughout the movie, or sit there and try to hide the fact that you are starting to like it. And, don't always wait for her to initiate in the relationship. As a matter of fact, initiation should be your default orientation when it comes to your marriage. You take the lead. It shows her that you care enough about her and your marriage to take the first step.

Physically — I have a friend of mine whose wife recently had neck surgery. When she came home from the procedure, although she was still mobile and relatively able to care for herself, he stepped up to the plate and cooked for her. He made sure she stayed on schedule with taking her meds and that she didn't over exert herself and got the rest she needed, and so forth. Now that's a good example of this point. But caring for our wives physically goes beyond when they are sick or recovering from surgery. We also demonstrate care for them in this area by supporting their fitness and wellness goals. Most women are concerned about how they feel and look–from their bodies to their hair to their wardrobe. As husbands, we should allow them the space they desire to do what they need to do—within reason of course—and encourage them to that end. At the same time though, we need to be careful not to impose pop culture's standard of beauty onto them. If you like a particular dress or hairstyle on your wife, or when she actively takes care of herself physically, by all means feel free to recommend or express that in love. But remember: there is more to our wives than meets the eye. So if your wife has put on an extra few pounds or doesn't look flawless every day, please don't turn a molehill into a mountain. At the end of the day, "Charm is deceitful, and beauty is vain, but a woman who fears the Lord is to be praised." (Proverbs 31:30)

Emotionally — I was completely oblivious to this aspect of caring for my wife when we were first married. It wasn't until she opened up and explained to me how she felt, that I realized I had been inadvertently neglecting to care for her in this regard. For instance, there were a few times my wife had run-ins with certain individuals and she would come home to talk about the situation. In the course of our discussion, I would, for the most part, give the other person the benefit of the doubt and express concern about how that person would feel or think if she confronted him or her in a certain way. And then I would proceed to encourage her to respond in a way that would reflect Christ. Doesn't sound too bad, right? Well, my wife, after becoming exasperated with me, finally shared how she felt I had more concern for the other person's feelings, or thoughts, than hers. After one altercation and becoming tired of being confused, I just asked her, "Honey, what's the problem? Because I don't understand why you are frustrated with me when I am simply trying to be objective and encourage you to handle this in a way that honors Jesus." To which she replied, "My issue has nothing to do with what you mentioned. I appreciate that about you. My problem is you never really acknowledge how I feel and what I think. I don't expect you to always agree with me, but I would like for you to at least communicate that you hear me and understand how I feel or think about the issue." Talk about a revelation! I hadn't even realized I was coming off that way to my wife, and how it seemed I didn't care about her feelings.

Showing sympathy is a weakness for many of us. Some of us see it as a waste of energy or as irrelevant because in our minds it doesn't lend to solving the problem. But hear this, brothers: If we solely play the role of fixer, we will find ourselves in a fix with our wives. Remember this general rule of thumb: sympathize first, solve second. And by the way, sympathizing with our spouses is not a weakness; it is a strength. Even Jesus, in serving as our great high priest, sympathizes with us when it comes to our weaknesses in temptations (yet he never sinned; Hebrews 5:14-15). So, let's embrace this Christ-like characteristic and sympathize with our wives, even if we don't fully relate to their experience.

Domestically — My late father never seemed to miss a teachable moment. I'll never forget the day I was sitting on my parent's couch watching television as a teenager. My father came home from a hard day's work and spoke to me as he walked towards his bedroom. After a few minutes, he came back into the living room and proceeded into the kitchen. With his dingy work clothes still on, he stood over the sink and began washing dishes. With his back still turned to me, he said, "EJ, one day, if the Lord says the same, you are going to get married. Do you see what I am doing? There is nothing wrong with you as a man coming home and helping your wife around the house. I could easily have just come home, plopped down on the couch like you and watched TV for the rest of the day. But a man pitches in wherever he can without having to be asked. Learn this now, son, before you get married. Your wife will appreciate it." Yeah, he slipped a gut punch in on me. But, point well taken. I know that some of our wives might have a particular way of doing things around the house and would prefer that we let them do it. Even if that is so, we can either learn how to do it her way, or look to help out with something else. Straighten up the room. Place the clothes in the washer or dryer, and, if she allows you to, fold and put them up when they are done. Vacuum the house. Cook or be her "sous chef." Make the bed. I am well aware that everyone's household doesn't operate the same or in the traditional sense with wives taking care of things inside the house, while the husbands handle everything on the outside. Variations do exist. Whatever the particulars might be in your marriage, the point still remains: don't leave your wife to do the house work alone. Get up and pitch in.

Parentally — "Listen, Pastor, I work hard to provide for my wife and kid(s). After a long, hard day on the job, I think I should be entitled to come home, put my feet up and watch ESPN, CNN, or HGTV. Don't get me wrong. I engage with my child when they are at home. But my role is primarily a provider, protector, and disciplinarian, while my wife is the hands-on one, a nurturer, comforter, and moral supporter. She's good at what she does. So I mainly leave the parenting thing to her." Again, please don't be that guy. And if you are, it's time to step up to the plate as a dad. Answer this question for me: From a biblical standpoint, whose primary responsibility is it to raise a child in the discipline and instruction of the Lord? That's right, fathers (Ephesians 6:4). This isn't to say that mothers get a pass on, or have no role to play in, rearing children. They are most definitely to be involved in parenting as well. But—in traditional settings where there are two parents, a father and a mother—we are to be the "resident pastors" at our residence. When we actively step into our God-given role, our wives will feel the love we have not only for our children but for them as well. So, practically, what does caring for our wives look like on the parental front? You put the kids down and let her relax. Take them out for a few hours or a whole day and give her a breather. You lovingly instruct and discipline your children and don't simply pass this baton on to your wife. You read to and play with them. And do not, I repeat, do not leave living a godly example before your children, reading the Bible to them, praying and going to church with them, and teaching them about the Good News of Jesus to your wife alone. You shepherd your child's heart to Jesus. You bear the majority of the weight of the blessed burden and privilege of parenting, and humbly accept the extraordinary and invaluable help that she provides as a mother. But don't invert this. As a byproduct, your wife will feel cared for as you joyfully and willingly carry out your fathering responsibility.

Socially — If your wife is a home body, encourage her to have some "me" time and to occasionally hang out with her friends/family. Or, if she expresses a desire to go on a rare outing with her girls or family, let her. If your wife truly understands God's design of marriage being that of leaving and cleaving, then I am certain she has already proven to you that you are her priority. So, in light of that, please don't be so stingy with your wife. Manipulating her feelings so that she will decline the invitation of girlfriends, family, or co-workers to hang out with them is not loving; it is selfish and conniving. Also, don't be controlling when it comes to your wife having cordial social interaction with people, specifically men, because of your lack of trust in them (I struggled with this when my wife and I were dating in college).

First, that is misplacing your trust. You don't have to trust other men; you just need to trust your wife's faithfulness to you and that she is wise and aware of her dealings with other guys, and will take heed to any warnings you may give her in relationship to them. Secondly, you can't control what other men feel, think, or do. It is an exercise in futility. So don't allow your trepidation to become your wife's incarceration. In other words, don't imprison your wife because of your insecurity. If she has given you no reason to be concerned about her social life, don't be. Trust her. She will appreciate you for it.

YouTube is probably not going anywhere anytime soon. If it is captured on video, you are more than likely to see it uploaded on this website for the world to see. There are those good, tear-jerker videos, like soldiers coming home from a tour of duty to surprise their unsuspecting family. And then there are the not-so-good ones. Street fights, soft pornography, glorification of drugs, and people being caught committing all other kinds of unlawful, unethical, and inappropriate acts. I ran across one such video a while back that serves as good illustrative material for this first overarching command to live with our wives in a caring manner. It featured a couple of employees who worked for a nationwide shipping company. As they were preparing to load packages into the truck, unbeknownst to them, they were being recorded by someone's dash cam. As the two employees talked, the male worker handed the female worker packages to place in the vehicle that were clearly to be handled with care. She, in turn, grabbed them and proceeded to throw these fragile contents into the delivery truck. The male worker felt emboldened by her actions and joined her in this reckless, irresponsible act; chunking boxes with no thought of their blatant violation of company policy and disregard for their customers' trust in them to properly handle their items. I am sure you see how this illustration applies to us as husbands. How are you handling your wife? Don't treat her like those employees did those packages. God has entrusted her to you and expects you to abide by his policy, the Bible, as it relates to her. Handle her with care.

We are commanded to honor our wives

As husbands, we desire for our wives to respect us, and rightly so. For Paul in Ephesians 5:33 commands our wives to do just that. But showing respect is not a one-way street because Peter directs us, in turn, to honor our wives: *"showing honor to the woman as the weaker vessel ... "* (1 Peter 3:7). They deserve our utmost respect. Honoring her can range from simple expressions of chivalry (e.g., opening the door for your wife to wearing a symbol of your covenant marriage–your wedding ring) to more substantial acts like those mentioned in chapter one. If you stop and think about it, I am sure you already know ways in which you can fulfill this command in relationship to your significant other. So instead of giving you the "how," I want to round out this chapter focusing on the "why." Why should you and I honor our wives? Peter answers this question for us in the latter part of verse seven of chapter three: "since they are heirs with you of the grace of life." I understand heirs of the grace of life to mean that by grace our wives—as it is with us—have been saved from sin and adopted as children into the family of God the Father through faith in Christ and consequently will inherit the blessing of life in heaven when Jesus returns to fully establish his eternal kingdom (Titus 3:4-7)[7]. Peter, under the assumption that we as Christian men are married to Christian women—which is God's ideal, by the way; but that's another point for another time—in essence says, we should honor our wives because their spiritual

---

[7] Some scholars believe that "heirs of the grace of life" is referring to the husband and wife sharing together in the grace of *married* life. I am not totally sold on this interpretation simply due to the fact that, in the Scriptures, the word heir is usually associated with a future inheritance, namely eternal life in the glories of heaven with our Triune God. Others interpret this to mean that wives are recipients of the grace of *physical* life just as their husbands and should therefore be respected as human beings created in the image of God.

position before God is the same as ours. We are not better than they are. We are not on a higher plane than them. We are all in the same spiritual bracket. We are sons and they are daughters of God – Daddy's girls.

If this is indeed what Peter meant by what he wrote, then this image of our Christian wives being God's daughters serves as a backdrop for Peter's last statement in verse seven: "so that your prayers are not hindered." Wait. What? No, your eyes are not playing tricks on you. You read it right. This is a divine deterrent to keep us away from not showing our wives the respect they are due. God says to us as husbands, I will block your prayers if you dishonor my daughters.

Let's say you have given your daughter's hand in marriage to a young man. One day your son-in-law comes to ask you for a personal favor, but you knew of his constant mistreatment of your daughter. Are you going to be more or less inclined to grant him his request? I would imagine you would be less inclined. So, don't be surprised if God denies your prayer requests as a direct result of disrespecting his daughter. Would you expect a perfect and good Heavenly Father to do otherwise?

Chapter 5

Where's Romeo?

Though they would not necessarily use the same verbiage, this is a question some wives wake up asking themselves after years of being married to their husbands. *"Where has the romance gone? He was so creatively romantic when we were dating. He used to sweep me off my feet with his caring and thoughtful gestures. Now everything just seems so perfunctory. There is this emotional distance between us. I feel like the fire has all but gone out in our marriage,"* they muse. To which some of us would reply, "I work hard to provide for her. If she wants something, for the most part and if it is within our means, she has the leeway to go and get it. She gets anniversary and birthday gifts from me every year. What more am I supposed to do? Life isn't one big honeymoon, you know." I understand completely. Yet the truth is, over time, the day-to-day grind has a way of buffering the romantic shine out of marriages if we let it. And that's when it is just the two of you. Just imagine what happens when kids enter the picture.

It would be great if our marriages reflected some of these television shows where a guy gets to whisk his girl off on weekly romantic dates to elegant restaurants, exclusive resorts and islands, and to engage in extravagant activities, all on someone else's dime. But that's not reality for the majority of us. However, that doesn't mean we are off the hook. Admittedly, we all can get caught in a romantic-less rut. And so my prayer is that God will use this chapter to energize those of us who have grown lethargic in this area and instruct all of us on how we can continue to stoke the flame of romance in our marriages from here on out.

Songs are mirrors, reflecting back to us the image of our lives. But they are also in some ways teachers, schooling us on various life topics. And one of the main subjects that songs–particularly the oldies, like Motown and R&B – teach us about is love, sex, and romance.

There is one song, however, that tops them all when it comes to this topic. It is the Song of Songs or the Song of Solomon. Although there are scholarly disputes as to the author of the book, one thing is for certain: the person who wrote this song—which is essentially a celebration of romantic love between men and women in the context of marriage—was divinely inspired. The author (who I believe to be King Solomon) had a "ghost writer"—God the Holy Spirit—who gave him the lyrics to this musical poem. There is no shortage of outlines of this book of the Bible. I decided to go with Dr. John MacArthur's[8]–he breaks the book up into three major sections: 1. The Courtship: "Leaving" (1:2-3:5), 2. The Wedding: "Cleaving" (3:6-5:1), and 3. The Marriage: "Weaving" (5:2-8:14)–primarily because, as you can see, it is simple to understand for the majority of us who are bottom-line-thinking type of guys. For our purpose, we are only going to look at a few verses in the last section. There are four gems buried within that I want to unearth, which I believe will help to enrich the romance in our marriages.

---

[8] John MacArthur, *"Grace to You,"* March 29, 2010, http://www.gty.org/resources/bible-introductions/MSB22/song-of-solomon

Befriend Your Wife Regularly

After taking a refreshing bath and settling herself in bed for the night, the wife, in chapter five of Song of Solomon, hears a knock at the door. (Apparently, some scholars believe, all of this is happening in a dream according to verse two—"I slept, but my heart was awake.") It's her husband who desires to come in so that he can be with his wife. Something doesn't appear right about their relationship because the wife gives some pretty weak excuses for why she doesn't get up to open the door for her husband: "I had put off my garment; how could I put it on? I had bathed my feet; how could I soil them?" (vs. 3) After failing at his attempt to open the door, the husband leaves the house (vs. 6). The wife, having a change of heart, goes out to try to find her husband. In doing so, she solicits the help of some women, the "daughters of Jerusalem" (vs. 8). The women respond by asking why they should go looking for her husband. What makes him more special than others? (vs. 9) The wife, in turn, gives this fairly lengthy response, describing and extolling her husband's looks (vs. 10-16a). But it was what she said about her husband to them at the end that caught my attention: *This is my beloved and this is my friend..."* (vs. 16b, emphasis mine).

She considered her husband to be not only her lover but her friend, her companion. Though the writer doesn't go into details (a musical poem is meant to highlight not explicate in detail the subject it speaks to), it is obvious that this gentleman loved being with his lady. He befriended her. And the same should be true of us. There's little else that speaks romance to a woman like a man who engages her as a person to be loved on and not just a body to be fondled with (which, by the way, is one of the devastating effects of the sin of pornography. It influences men to objectify women, seeing them simply as bodies to be sexually exploited rather than as people to be respectfully treated.). Befriending your wife shouldn't only be seen as something you did in courtship days to win her over, but also as something you do continuously in your marriage now. If the flame of romance is to keep burning in our marriages, we must befriend our wives regularly.

Delving deep into this point to establish an extensive list of practical steps on how to befriend your wife, would probably be counterproductive. For one, most of us already know what to do. We just need to do it and keep it up. And two, befriending our mates will more than likely vary from marriage to marriage. Sure there are some similarities, but even within that there are still nuances particular to how you and your wife do things. But, for those who don't know what befriending their wives would entail, my recommendation to you is simple: ask them to give you some idea of what activities they enjoy, or think they would enjoy taking part in with you. Listen and take mental notes. Do it and then repeat. And add some variety in there from time to time to keep it fresh.

Adore Your Wife's Physical Features

Some of the similes the writer employs in relationship to his wife more than likely don't resonate with many of us today because the objects he compares her to are specific to his location, time, and culture. For example, he writes,

> "You are beautiful as Tirzah, my love, lovely as Jerusalem, awesome as an army with banners." (6:4)

> "Your hair is like a flock of goats leaping down the slopes of Gilead." (6:5b)

> "Your teeth are like a flock of ewes that have come up from the washing; all of them bear twins; not one among them has lost its young." (6:6)

> "Your neck is like an ivory tower." (7:4a)

Tirzah (an old Canaanite city) and Jerusalem, as ancient cities during the period of Old Testament history, were known at the time for their immaculate buildings and beautiful surroundings. A flock of goats. Well, for us city guys, we probably haven't seen anything like that; maybe one goat at a zoo, but definitely not a flock of goats. We may not fully comprehend the references and imagery in the poem, but what he is doing is absolutely clear and ought to be replicated in our marriages: he adores his wife's physical features.

As I stated earlier, there is absolutely more to your wife than her body, but that doesn't mean the body is unimportant. Our physical bodies are not just shells that house the important part of us: our souls. They are inextricably tied to our humanity (God made us body and soul/spirit). We shouldn't obsess over them, but neither should we disregard them. For those of us who do the former, I want to challenge you to dial it back some. Unfortunately too many of us have a narrow and shallow stereotypical view of physical beauty that has been shaped by women we have seen on television, in theaters, in magazines, or in person; which has sadly caused some of us to become discontented with our wives' physical makeup, leading us to place undue and unhealthy pressure on them to conform to those images. On the other hand, there is nothing wrong with encouraging our wives to take care of themselves and making known to them what appeals to us concerning their appearance (and the same is true for them in relationship to us). But we need to ensure it is coming from a pure place in our hearts and not from some fleshly, worldly and misguided notion of physical beauty and sexuality. And whatever you do, for those to whom this applies, don't compare the woman who you are with now to the one(s) you've been with in the past. Your wife has been fearfully and wonderfully made by God. Therefore, she is unique and has her own standard of beauty.

So, what do you appreciate and like about your wife's looks? Don't just think about it. Tell her, and be specific. Did she just get her hair done at the beauty salon? Make sure you take notice and compliment her. Does she have a smile that lights up your heart when you see it? Say so. When she looks at you with those eyes, does it cause your heart to race? Yes? Then let her know about it. How about her lips? Do they just do something for you? Good. Now share that with her. There is more I could say, but I'll just keep it above the neck. Anything below that, well, you can handle it.

Enjoy Your Wife Sexually

> "Your stature is like a palm tree, and your breasts are like its clusters. I say I will climb the palm tree and lay hold of its fruit." (7:7-8a)

Yes, that is a verse in the Bible. And, yes, it is in reference to physical intimacy and sex. God created this most intimate physical act to be a mutually enjoyable experience between one man and one woman who have joined together in covenant marriage. When it is spoken of in that light, it is celebrated as good and right. There is no guilt and shame associated with it at all.

But what does this have to do with keeping the romance ablaze in marriage? Admittedly, sex in marriage can become, to a good degree, a one-sided ordeal if we let it; that is, where we primarily look to have our wives meet *our* sexual desires. We can be selfish in this area of our marriages as we can with any other. Yet, when you and I exhibit appropriate personal sexual satisfaction with our wives, we are saying to them: "You are enough for me." Mark it down: sexual monogamy enhances relational intimacy. Assuming the reality of both husband and wife being rightly related to God in Christ and living life submitted to the Holy Spirit and according to the Bible, when we are committed to being sexually content with our wives, they will in turn feel and respond like the woman in the Song of Solomon: "I am my beloved's, and his desire is for me." (7:10)

Feel free to wholeheartedly and lavishly enjoy your wife sexually and, if I might add, look to please her as well. Remember, brothers, we are like those old muzzle-loaded musket rifles. We only have one round to work with at a time. Once we fire off, we are done...at least until we reload, which normally takes a minute. She is an automatic pistol with a 15-round magazine. Pull her trigger a few times.

Keep The Lord Jesus And His Gospel At The Center Of Your Life And Marriage

Fire is a common image in the Bible that is used metaphorically to speak of God's activity of cleansing his people from sin (Malachi 3:2-3) or of God's judgment or wrath (Psalm 21:9; 78:21; 89:46). Some time ago, I was asked to speak at a men's conference on the subject of love, sex, and romance. In my preparation leading up to the event, I discovered that the Scripture also employs the element of fire to refer to that very topic, namely, passionate love, or, as it is more popularly stated, romance. But there's more. Not only does the Bible picture romance as a flame, it also identifies its source: "Set me as a seal upon your heart, as a seal upon your arm, for love is strong as death, jealousy [or passion] is fierce as the grave. Its flashes are flashes of fire, *the very flame of the LORD*" (Song of Solomon 8:6, emphasis mine). There are at least three implications to this truth. First, since God created human romance, it should therefore be embraced, without reservation, as good and wholesome. Secondly, it should only be experienced in the God-approved confines of covenant marriage between one man and one woman. Thirdly, we must recognize the Lord Jesus as being the source of the flame of romance and commit to handling it the way he desires. If we don't, we will run the risk of either becoming consumed by it: where we idolize our wives, placing our identity and worth in them instead of Jesus, which spawns some ungodly, ugly, and unhealthy tendencies like controlling manipulation, sinful jealousy, and abuse; or being haphazard with it: where we commit blazing acts of adultery, leaving our wives and children burned and smoldering in hurt, anger, bitterness, and disillusionment.

In year two of our marriage, my wife and I found ourselves moving from Waco to Dallas, TX, as I was just hired on to work in the position that I am in today at the church where I serve. We had signed the contract on our new home and received the keys. Having lived in a two bedroom, one bath duplex, to now moving into a two-story, three bedroom, two bathrooms house as first-time home buyers, you can imagine our excitement. From the extra square footage to the large patio to the sprawling back yard, there was much we liked about the house. There was one feature about our house that we especially came to love: the fireplace. When you take into consideration that we had vaulted ceilings, only one A/C unit that serviced the whole house and what our electricity bill was during the winter months (one winter a few of our bills were over $500...consecutively!), I am sure you understand why we cherished it.

On those cold winter nights, we had an alternative and more cost-effective way to heat up our living room where we hung out as a family in the evening. As long as the fire was properly started, contained, and maintained in its appropriate context–the fireplace–it was good for us. To do otherwise would have invited great harm to not only our house but to our lives as well. The same is true of the flame of romance. For it to burn white hot and serve as a benefit to you and your wife it must be started, maintained, and contained in its proper context: the fireplace of marriage. Not doing so will cause the flame of your love to turn into a wild forest fire, damaging everything in its path.

When we, through prayerful dependence on the Holy Spirit, keep Jesus at the center of our lives and marriages, he will ensure that the flame of romance stays in its marital fireplace and will never be snuffed out.

Chapter 6

Faithful unto Death

L et me put the cards on the table upfront. Faithfulness to our wives is not contingent upon what they do or don't do. Ultimately, the decision to remain faithful or to violate our marriage covenant by stepping out on them to be with another woman (or in some cases, with another man. I had to mention this because, whether we acknowledge it or not, it is a reality of the day and time in which we live) falls on us. *"Well, maybe if we had more sex or if she would have been more exploratory with me in bed, then I wouldn't have…"* I hear you, but that's not a justifiable reason. *"The reason I stepped out on her was because she didn't respect me as her husband."* Unfortunate, but yet still invalid. Without a doubt, the condition of that type of marriage can be very challenging to live with, which is why I devote the next chapter to dealing with this reality. But committing adultery is not the way to cope with or alleviate the frustration, anger, and hurt you may feel. On the other end of the spectrum, you have those men who were in good marriages–whose wives respected them, submitted to their loving leadership, were madly in love with them, and made sure they willingly fulfilled their part of the conjugal duty of marriage–but still got caught up in an adulterous affair. Whether we are talking about a healthy or unhealthy marriage, if we are going to be faithful unto death, we must understand that adultery doesn't ultimately happen due to circumstances outside of us, but rather from corruption on the inside of us.

THE HEART OF THE MATTER

While conversing with the Pharisees and scribes about their issue with his disciples not keeping the elders' tradition of washing their hands before eating and confronting their hypocrisy of honoring God with their lips but laying aside the commandment of God for the traditions of men, Jesus took the opportunity to teach the crowd about where true spiritual defilement originates from:

> *"And he called the people to him again and said to them, 'Hear me, all of you, and understand: There is nothing outside a person that by going into him can defile him, but the things that come out of a person are what defile him.' And when he had entered the house and left the people, his disciples asked him about the parable. And he said to them, 'Then are you also without understanding? Do you not see that whatever goes into a person from outside cannot defile him, since it enters not his heart but his stomach, and is expelled?' (Thus he declared all foods clean.) And he said, 'What comes out of a person is what defiles him.* **For from within, out of the heart of man,** *come evil thoughts, sexual immorality, theft, murder,* adultery, *coveting, wickedness, deceit, sensuality, envy, slander, pride, foolishness. All these evil things come from within, and they defile a person.'"* (Mark 7:14-23; emphasis mine)

And there it is. Adultery comes from within. It's not that there aren't any external factors that can contribute to us acting unfaithfully, but the fundamental cause of infidelity, as Jesus said, is rooted in the heart; or what Paul calls in his writings "the flesh"—the proclivity to sin connected to our old, sinful life which still seeks to infringe upon our new life in Christ. This is why we need to constantly remind ourselves and be reminded of the gospel of Jesus; that "those who belong to Christ Jesus have crucified the flesh with its passions and desires" (Galatians 5:24) and are now able, through the indwelling Holy Spirit, to not allow sin to reign in our mortal bodies, to make us obey its passions (Romans 6:12; cf. also to Romans 8:1-13).

To live faithfully with our wives until we breathe our last breath is not obtained simply by mustering up the strength to daily suppress our lustful desires. That would be utterly exhausting because the allure of sin is beyond our capacity to withstand. We must instead meditate on the glorious truth of our Savior's total and sufficient death on the cross for our sins, which absorbed all of God's righteous wrath against us, absolved us of all sin, purchased our redemption, and rendered the slavish power of sin over our lives ineffective. Paul stated it this way, "We know that our old self was crucified with him in order that the body of sin might be brought to nothing, so that we would no longer be enslaved to sin" (Romans 6:6).

But there is also the twin work of our salvation: Jesus' resurrection from the dead. If Jesus' death liberated us from sin, then his resurrection enslaved us to righteousness, which produces sanctification ending in the free gift of eternal life in Christ Jesus (Romans 6:18-19, 22-23). Because of Jesus' triumphant resurrection from the dead we who trust in him can walk in the newness of life (Romans 6:4). This new walk means we now desire to live our lives according to God's standards and adhere to His wisdom. It is a wisdom that enlightens us to the fact that there are in fact dangers outside of us that seek to entice the sinful desires within us to violate God's command and our marriage covenant, and instructs us accordingly. To this wisdom we now turn.

THE FORBIDDEN WOMAN

I love the book of Proverbs. Rooted in the fear of the Lord, it gives practical, down-to-earth, rubber-meets-the-road wisdom for life. These divinely inspired pithy axioms, for the most part, are not ironclad promises or guarantees from God. But, generally speaking, people who seek to follow them tend to live more productive, meaningful, and peaceful lives. Solomon, who authored the majority of the proverbs (Proverbs 1:1), covers a wide range of topics: from warning us of the trouble an unbridled tongue produces, to the unwise decision of indiscriminately serving as co-signers on another person's loan. Out of all that Solomon addressed there was one subject matter he spoke about extensively and repeatedly in the first few chapters of Proverbs, namely adultery. As a father giving sound advice to his married son, Solomon warns him—and, by extension, us as well–of the temptation and consequences of infidelity. Those who find themselves caught in adultery often times walk straight into a trap, a well-camouflaged one that sets before them the bait of emotional, relational, sexual gratification but hides the destruction it will cause to their marriages and lives. In Proverbs chapter five, Solomon brushes away the foliage to expose what is really there. He speaks candidly about the characteristics of who he calls the forbidden[9] woman, a "Dirty Diana"[10], a groupie of sorts, if you will, in hopes that we don't fall prey to her.

---

[9] The Hebrew word here has a few denotations, among which are "unauthorized person," "strange woman or harlot," and "the other". I prefer the ESV rendering of "forbidden" here because it keeps the term broad enough so as not to restrict its application to that, for example, of a prostitute, which would incidentally give men room to wrongly imply that adultery is therefore permissible with anyone else.

[10] "Dirty Diana" is the ninth track on Michael Jackson's seventh album, *Bad*.

She is seductive

I find it interesting here in this passage Solomon doesn't make mention of her physical attractiveness but rather her speech as being seductive. This is perceptive of Solomon because not all men are seduced by looks at first, or alone. Some men, and to a degree all of us, can be wooed into committing adultery based on a woman's words. Think about it. Let's say a friend of yours comes home to a wife who berates and belittles him. She doesn't speak lovingly and respectfully to him. She is brutal and careless with her words, or she rarely, if ever, verbally applauds him. But then he goes to work, to the gym, or onto social media and runs into a woman who takes an interest in him and begins to shower him with pleasantries. Over time, a fondness grows between them and one thing leads to the next. He comes to confide in you about what he has done. After talking a few times, your curiosity gets the best of you. So you ask to see a picture of this woman. And when you do, you are dumbfounded as to how she, comparatively speaking, doesn't even look as good as his wife. Still befuddled, you go and talk to your dude, "Say man, this girl you've been messing around with; she doesn't even begin to hold a candle to your wife. Your wife is gorgeous, bro. I'm confused. You are going to have to help me with this one because I don't understand how you could leave what you have for that." To which he responds, "It doesn't really have anything to do with how she looks. I mean, she's not bad looking. But yeah, my wife blows her out of the water when it comes to the physical feature department, not to even mention her intelligence, personality, heart, giving spirt, and other aspects of who she is. But, unlike my wife, she took an interest in me. It was what she said that drew me to her. She respected me. She admired me. And I fell for her. . .I fell for her."

Solomon writes, "For the lips of a forbidden woman drip honey, and her speech is smoother than oil" (Proverbs 5:3). She knows what and how to say things that are sweet and soothing to your heart as a man. And her timing is almost impeccable. "But in the end," Solomon warns, "she is bitter as wormwood, sharp as a two-edged sword" (Proverbs 5:4)[11]. Did you notice the contrasts in verses three and four? Whereas in the beginning of the illicit relationship her words are like honey, but after you consume them and have your fill of her, she and her words will leave a bitter taste in your mouth. When the affair first jumps off, her speech is smoother than oil, but when it is all said and done, she and her words will wound you like a razor sharp two-edged sword. Adultery, at first, will bring delight to your relational palate, but in the end it will be distasteful and will deaden your conscience, your judgment and your decisions. And it will severely damage your marriage.

She is deadly

Solomon continues his sobering description of this adulterous woman, "Her feet go down to death; her steps follow the path of Sheol" (Proverbs 5:5). "That woman will be the death of you," is how we might say it today. And in some cases that literally can become a reality. Ever heard of persons murdering their spouses' adulterous partners or their unfaithful spouses themselves, or even the adulterous lover killing the unfaithful spouse with whom he or she had a relationship, all out of a jealous rage? But there are other ways in which you can experience death if you go down that path of adultery with this forbidden woman; one, for example, being the death of your wife's trust in you. Another one would be the death of your marriage. You need to know not all marriages recover from such a devastating betrayal. Divorce

---

11 Wormwood is "a plant toward two feet high, belonging to the Genus *Artemisia* (Spec. *Artemisia absinthium*), which produces a very firm stalk with many branches, grayish leaves, and small, almost round, pendent blossoms. It has a bitter and saline taste, and seems to have been regarded in the East as also a poison, of which the frequent combination with שׁאר gives an intimation." Lange, J. P., Schaff, P., Zöckler, O., & Aiken, C. A. (2008). *A commentary on the Holy Scriptures: Proverbs* (p. 77). Bellingham, WA: Logos Bible Software.

is a real and possible consequence of stepping outside of God's marital boundary.

She is careless

"She doesn't ponder the path of life; her ways wander; and she does not [or you don't] know it" (Song of Solomon 5:6). She doesn't hold to the righteous road of God's word. She, honestly, couldn't care less about it, particularly as it relates to its prohibition of not being in a romantic relationship with you, a married man. She, or you, may not realize it—especially when you are entangled in a full-on adulterous relationship and everything feels right, good, and straight—but her ways (her flirting, her pursuit of you, her seemingly innocent adoration of you, her fantasies about you, etc.) are crooked. They are dangerously tempting and sinful. What is also so insidious about her is she will even say she cares about you, but in all actuality she doesn't; because if she did, she would respect your wife who is one with you. If she doesn't honor your wife and the covenant between you two, she doesn't truly care for you, no matter what she says to the contrary.

Solomon now turns in verses seven through nineteen of Proverbs chapter five to give us some wise instructions on how we can adultery-proof our marriages. He doesn't give us ten ways to do this, for which we should be grateful; otherwise it would be too complex for us to achieve. He essentially encourages us to take heed to two pieces of practical advice:

1. Distance yourself from the forbidden woman.

Stay *far* away from her, and her residence as well (Proverbs 5:8). We don't need to be anywhere near her nor where she hangs out; whether that be her apartment, house, cubicle, office, the tennis court, gym, online video chat sites, etc. Now I am not trying to be extreme or legalistic here. Sure you and I, for example, can continue going to the gym that we frequent, even though we know there is a chance that she might show up. But when she enters, we need to exit. Having said that though, there may be times when it would be most advantageous and wise for us to just change gyms altogether. The point is, mind your proximity. The closer you are to her the more precarious the temptation becomes. As far as it depends on you, steer clear of her.

To further instill the virtue of marital fidelity in his sons, Solomon speaks to them about the consequences of not obeying his counsel to keep far away from an adulteress. He writes, "lest you give your honor to others and your years to the merciless, lest strangers take their fill of your strength, and your labors go to the house of a foreigner" (Proverbs 5:9-10). If you take time to think about these two verses and look around at some men who have committed adultery, or maybe even yourself, and the subsequent fallout, you will discover Solomon hit the bull's eye dead center. Men who are caught in, or confess to, adultery lose respect. They experience grief due to those who are bent on making their lives a living hell; be it a scorned wife, or an obsessed lover. They lose their vitality in some measure, and as mentioned earlier, perhaps some even lose their lives. And their wealth grows wings and flies away. How so? The text is silent because it could happen in a number of ways:

> He gets blackmailed and has to pay to keep the other woman or women quiet

> He spends money on the one with whom he is committing adultery (e.g., dinners, hotel rooms, gifts, paying her rent/mortgage/car payment, etc.)

> He ends up having a baby with the other woman and now has to pay child support

> He pays for the service of an escort

> He goes into debt, using a secret credit card to fund his addiction to pornography

There are more examples I could give, but you get the drift. Adultery might be exhilarating at the outset, but it will prove to be debilitating in the end. If we travel on this road of adultery, we will eventually have a head-on collision with regret and agony, "...and at the end of your life you groan, when your flesh and body are consumed, and you say, 'How I hated discipline, and my heart despised reproof! I did not listen to the voice of my teachers or incline my ear to my instructors. I am at the brink of utter ruin in the assembled congregation.'" (Proverbs 5:11-14)

2. Delight yourself in your wife.

Whereas in Proverbs chapter five verses seven through fourteen, we were instructed to refrain from adultery, now in Proverbs chapter five verses fifteen through nineteen we are exhorted to relish in sexual intimacy with our wives only. Solomon uses figurative language here to paint a vivid picture of not only our moral responsibility before God to be faithful to our wives, but also of the accompanying sexual gratification that comes from such a monogamous relationship.

Quench Your Thirst

Solomon directs us to "Drink water from your own cistern, flowing water from your own well" (Proverbs 5:15). Both the drinking of water and flowing water is figurative language for sexual pleasure, and the cistern and well represent our wives. He then turns to ask an interrogative question in verse sixteen, "Should your springs be scattered abroad, streams of water in the streets?" The expected answer is no. So, he concludes in verse seventeen, "Let them be for yourself alone, and not for strangers with you." We should look to have our sexual needs met by our wives and no one else. Our wives are the only legitimate means for quenching our sexual thirst.

Drunk in Love

Have you ever seen someone who had a little bit too much to drink? You can easily tell when a person is full off of an alcoholic beverage. All of his faculties are affected in some way. Slurred speech. Staggered walk. Blurred sight. Forgetful memory. Far from glorifying the sin of drunkenness and its negative effects, Solomon takes this idea of being inebriated and uses it positively to speak about our need to be drunk in marital love and intimacy when he writes, "Let her breasts fill you at all times with delight; be intoxicated always in her love" (Proverbs 5:19). We ought to be so joyfully captivated by the beauty of our wives ("Let your fountain be blessed, and rejoice in the wife of your youth, a lovely deer, a graceful doe." Proverbs 5:18-19a) and completely consumed romantically and sexually with them that the forbidden woman becomes a blur to us. Being sexually satisfied with your spouse will help prevent you from straying to the other woman's house.

A SOBERING REALITY

"Why should you be intoxicated, my son, with a forbidden woman and embrace the bosom of an adulteress?" (Proverbs 5:20) On the heels of this rhetorical question—stated, I believe, with a tone of absurdity: With all that I have described to you in terms of the consequences of adultery and with all that you have at home in your wife, why in the world would you go hook up with another woman?—Solomon gives us the principal reason for why we should not commit such a sin: "For a man's ways are before the eyes of the Lord, and he ponders all his paths" (Proverbs 5:21). What a staggering thought. God is fully aware of everything we do, even those things we attempt to keep secret from our spouses, family, friends, church members, pastors, or anyone else. From the pornographic internet sites we peruse to the meticulously planned rendezvous with the mistress to the fantasies we journey on in our minds regarding other women, God sees it all. If you and I need a deterrent from sin, this theological truth definitely serves as one.

As Solomon concludes chapter five of Proverbs, he comes full circle to repeat the end results of one who breaks his marital covenant. The bleak reality is short and to the point. A man who fails to be disciplined in faithfulness to his wife and foolishly gets caught up in adultery will stagger to his own demise. The superficial delight of adultery is not worth the substantial devastation it will cause to your life, marriage and other relationships. To please God, to honor your wife, and to save yourself a lot of heartache and pain, stay faithful until death.

Chapter 7

Living in a Difficult Marriage

"M en are rational. Women are emotional." So the saying goes. But I don't completely buy that after seeing brothers who have come through my office with their wives to receive biblical counseling. Some wore their emotions on their sleeves, visibly displaying their pain or anger; while others attempted to suppress or dismiss them due to wrongly equating manhood with machoism. Regardless of how they handled their emotions, one thing was for certain, these men were worn down by having to live in a difficult marriage. Of course they committed their share of sins and mistakes in the marriage. But these guys readily owned up to them, humbly repented to God and their wives and were making the necessary changes. And yet their wives were vindictively holding it over their heads. Or, there were those instances when the wives were saying or doing things that were injurious to their husbands and to the marriage; some of which were due to being severely mistreated by other guys in past relationships, or to just their brazen and selfish desire to commit sin. You also had those men who were having a very challenging time dealing with their wives being adherents of another religion or atheistic worldview, or with their Christian wives who strongly held to unbiblical convictions or were living carnally. If any of that which I just mentioned—or some variation of it – applies to your marriage now, then this chapter is for you.

There is no way that I could address every single scenario you might be dealing with in your respective marriages. For one, there are varying dynamics of each relationship and particulars to each situation that require their own response. And two, to attempt to do so would turn this into a mammoth of a project; way more than seven chapters for sure. So I simply want to offer you some guiding principles that prayerfully will aid you in navigating the stormy marital waters you are in.

See your own sinfulness

When faced with your spouse's brokenness, it is sometimes easy to forget your own or to see her sinfulness as more egregious than yours. Doing either of these can cause you to become self-righteously judgmental, harsh, hypercritical, prideful, and impatient towards your wife. Whether your significant other is a non-Christian or a Christian who is acting carnal, your first order of business is not to look at her, but rather to do what I call, gospel introspection. This is where you think on how sinful you were (and still are in some respects; you and I have not arrived and are a work in progress), and how in spite of that God still saved you by grace through faith in the redemptive work of Jesus. And please, whatever you do, don't fall prey to the comparison game, where you try and stack up your depravity – or morality – against your wife's in order to view yourself in a better light than her.

This is why, when you do this gospel self-examination, you need to see yourself through the objective lens of the word of God and not through your subjective perspective. Read carefully what the Scripture says about all of us when we were in our pre-Christian state: "And you were dead in the trespasses and sins in which you once walked, following the course of this world, following the prince of the power of the air, the spirit that is now at work in the sons of disobedience—among whom we all once lived in the passions of our flesh, carrying out the desires of the body and the mind, and were by nature children of wrath, like the rest of mankind." (Ephesians 2:1-3) Paul continues, "But God, being rich in mercy, because of the great love with which he loved us, even when we were dead in our trespasses, made us alive together with Christ—by grace you have been saved…" (Ephesians 2:4). Not only do you need to presently look at your life in Christ, in comparison to your wife, and say, "But by the grace of God, there go I"; you must also remember your past life before Christ, in comparison to your wife, and say, "But by the grace of God, that is me." When you understand that what she is now you once were then, that the grace of God in Christ rescued you from sin and the just wrath of God to come, and how he continues to be patient and forgiving even when you sin now as his child, you will be more inclined to do the same in relationship to your wife (Colossians 3:12).

Don't long for greener pastures

When you find yourself in a very challenging marriage, the temptation to want to be with someone else can become even more pronounced and appealing. Coupled with that can come feelings and thoughts of contempt and discontentment towards your wife. In moments like these you need to seek God for truth, guidance, and strength. You need his perspective on the matter more than your own or anyone else's. Given your particular situation, you really can't trust your feelings because they are so jaded. God's word is sufficient to strengthen you when you are weak from dealing with trouble and temptation; and it illuminates the direction you should go – in terms of your thinking and your actions – when your pathway is dark (Psalm 119:28; 119:105).

So related to this point of not longing for greener pastures, there is one Scripture I want to highlight for you, especially part "a" of the verse: "Let marriage be held in honor among all, and let the marriage bed be undefiled, for God will judge the sexually immoral and adulterous" (Hebrews 13:4). Marriage should be valued and celebrated especially among us as Christians, regardless of what the conditions might be in our respective marriages. Why? Because it is a sacred institution established by God. This alone is reason enough for you to honor your covenant, even if being married to your wife has become cumbersome. For better or *for worse*, remember? Is it tough? Yes. Are there times when you feel like throwing in the towel? Of course. But listen, brother, marriage is meant to be for a lifetime. Honoring your marriage – even when it hurts to do so – honors God.

What will help you, in part, to not long for greener pastures is if you stay busy tending to your grass at home. Sometimes with suffering in marriage you can become passive or neutral towards your wife as a means of coping (e.g., by not wanting to deal with conflict at all so as to not get yourself worked up or get into a heated argument with her, or by refusing to bend over backwards again to do right by her when she does you wrong). But I want to encourage you to stay active towards her in ways that line up with God's word. Don't fall back from her out of spite. Lean in to her in love. Not necessarily because she loves you, but because God leaned in towards you, loving you supremely through Christ Jesus while you were yet a sinner (1 John 4:19; Romans 5:8).

Lastly, instead of lamenting over what your wife lacks, look at what attracted you to her in the first place. What are those God-engraved qualities about her you appreciate and admire?

Concentrate on that. It's not that you don't notice or are to simply ignore the weeds. But, you don't want to get so fixated on them to the point where you fail to see why you chose the yard that is your wife in the first place.

Remove divorce from the table

Unfortunately, too often divorce is the first option for many followers of Jesus when their marriages are on the rocks. But, according to Jesus, barring sexual immorality (an umbrella term which includes all forms of sexual sin: pornography, homosexuality, adultery, etc.), you have to hang in there and work, by God's grace, to better your marriage. And even in the case of sexual immorality, it is not an unforgiveable sin. With genuine repentance, and its accompanying fruit of obedience to God and faithfulness to spouse, marital reconciliation is possible.

And if you are married to an unbeliever, then that presents its own set of challenges, like conflicting beliefs, competing worldviews, and opposing sets of values. This doesn't mean you won't, and don't, agree on anything. But at the core of what you believe and who you are, you two are like night and day, or oil and water. This obviously can create a fair amount of tension and conflict in your marriage. And although that may be the case, divorce is not to be considered by you, the believing spouse, particularly when your unbelieving wife desires to stay married. This directive is given by Paul in 1 Corinthians 7:12-16 where he writes,

> "To the rest I say (I, not the Lord) that if any brother has a wife who is an unbeliever, and she consents to live with him, he should not divorce her. If any woman has a husband who is an unbeliever, and he consents to live with her, she should not divorce him. For the unbelieving husband is made holy because

of his wife, and the unbelieving wife is made holy because of her husband. Otherwise your children would be unclean, but as it is, they are holy. But if the unbelieving partner separates, let it be so. In such cases the brother or sister is not enslaved. God has called you to peace. For how do you know, wife, whether you will save your husband? Or how do you know, husband, whether you will save your wife?"

If you are married to an unbeliever[12] who consents to live with you, don't get a divorce (If she initiates the divorce, which Paul recognized is a possibility, then that's a different story. Let her go and move on with your life.). Remaining married will allow you to continue to influence her towards Jesus as she observes your devotion to him and your markedly different way of life and benefits, to some degree, from the blessings that come in this present life from your relationship with God.

As a general rule of thumb, divorce should not be our first and only option in a difficult marriage. Remove it from the table.

Go get counseling

For some guys, going to get counseling is equivalent to, say, going to get a root canal. There are brothers who seriously dislike the whole notion of going to someone outside of their marriage to speak to issues going on in their marriage. If that is you, I have a few remarks to make about this that will hopefully encourage

---

[12] This is not to imply that it is permissible for believers to knowingly marry unbelievers. How this was a reality with some in the Corinthian church was probably due to both the husband and wife being unbelievers when they first were married and sometime after that one of the spouses was saved by Jesus. Thus making for a mixed marriage. Believing singles should not willingly enter into marriage with unbelievers, which, I believe, is a legitimate application of the principle Paul gives in 2 Corinthians 6:14, "Do not be unequally yoked with unbelievers. For what partnership has righteousness with lawlessness? Or what fellowship has light with darkness?"

you to take advantage of this ministry. I call it a ministry because I am of the opinion that in order for counseling to be beneficial to a believing couple it should be conducted in a distinctly Christ-centered context with a mature Christian sitting across the table poised to aid them in viewing their relationship, roles, responsibilities, and responses through the lens of Scripture.

I hope you didn't miss a key three-letter word in that last sentence: aid. All of us need help with our marriages from time to time. Sometimes you need someone to serve as a referee who can ensure you fight fairly *for* your marriage because, if left to fend for yourselves in regards to that volatile issue, you would otherwise fight poorly *against* your marriage.

Counseling also is a benefit to you and your wife because it provides a third party who is able to more objectively assess your marital problem(s) and offer biblical solutions. Additionally, the counselor is there to encourage you all to see things from the other person's perspective and make whatever appropriate personal and relational adjustments to enhance your marriage, especially when you are (or she is, or both of you are) selfishly and stubbornly at odds over things like deeply entrenched personal preferences, behavioral tendencies, or approaches to handling conflict.

Proverbs 24:5-6 says, "A wise man is full of strength, and a man of knowledge enhances his might, for by wise guidance you can wage your war, and in abundance of counselors there is victory." Now if wise guidance can give a man the advantage in war, surely it can put your marriage in a position to win. Wise counselors can shed light on aspects of your marriage that you are in the dark about and will direct you, by God's word, to align yourself with God's will for you in relationship to your wife; and vice versa.

So humble yourself, and as far as it depends on you, be willing to get the help you and your wife need so that your marriage can have a chance to thrive.

Pray for your wife

One of the most spiritually effective acts you can do for your wife is to pray for her. I am aware for some this might seem like an exercise in futility because you have been praying and there has been little to no change in your wife. But there can be many variables as to why this is so: our motives are selfish, our expectations as to when and how God should answer our prayers are rigid, our faith is weak, our treatment of our wives is cruel, our requests are not in accord with God's word, or our wives' unwillingness to submit to the Lordship of Jesus in saving faith or in sanctifying obedience in some area(s) of their lives.

In spite of all of that, may this promise of Scripture strengthen your confidence in God and your commitment to pray for your wife during this difficult season in your marriage: "And this is the confidence that we have toward him, that if we ask anything according to his will he hears us. And if we know that he hears us in whatever we ask, we know that we have the requests that we have asked of him." (1 John 5:14-15)

Persevere in prayer for your wife, and pray for her according to God's will as it has been revealed to us in the Scriptures. And trust our infinitely wise, good, and sovereign God to answer your prayers regarding your wife in his own time and in his own way. And while you are at it, be sure to pray for yourself as well.

Look to Jesus

"Our marriage is in trouble. My wife is not who you think she is or who she portrays herself to be to you and others on Sunday morning. She is evil." Those were virtually the words spoken to me in passing by a dear brother in the Lord who was going through a very tumultuous time in his marriage. That might sound a bit dramatic, but that is the only way he could express it at the time. Although I had no reason not to believe his statements about his wife and the condition of their marriage, I took what he said with a grain of salt, not having had the opportunity to hear his wife's side of the story – which unfortunately never happened because she refused to come in for counseling. To be fair though, he didn't put all the blame on her. He readily acknowledged his failures and sins in the marriage, spoke of his repentance of them and the changes he had made and was making, by God's grace. As we spoke, it became apparent to me that though he had made some sinful, careless and unwise decisions, they didn't warrant the level of hardship his wife was supposedly putting him through at that moment.

For some of you who are reading this, that brother's situation is almost similar to what you are going through now in your home. So what are you to do in those times when you are either directly or indirectly suffering unjustly at the hands of your spouse? Turn your eyes to Jesus. This is basically what Peter writes to the persecuted believers in the five regions of Asia Minor who were living in tough, hostile social conditions. In addressing Christian servants who were working for unjust masters, Peter gives a needed and encouraging word, one that is applicable to marriage as well. He writes,

> "But if when you do good and suffer for it you endure, this is a gracious thing in the sight of God. For to this you have been called, because Christ also suffered for you, leaving you an example, so that you might follow in his steps. He committed no sin, neither was deceit found in his mouth. When he was reviled, he did not revile in return; when he suffered, he did not threaten, but continued entrusting himself to him who judges justly." (1 Peter 2:20b-23)

According to this passage of Scripture, we must understand to do good and endure mistreatment without retaliation is: 1. a commendable thing according to God because it reflects the grace he bestowed upon us sinners through the unjust suffering of his Son and our Savior Jesus on the cross for our sins; 2. a calling of every one of us who has placed saving faith in Christ and is now expected to follow in his footsteps by taking up the cross of sacrifice and suffering for his honor and for the good of others; and 3. a continual entrustment of ourselves to the One who sees all and will righteously judge all.

If you need a reason or motivation to endure in a difficult marriage, look to Jesus. If anyone understands what it is like to love someone who acts unloving towards you, it's Jesus. If anyone knows what it is like to do good to someone who treats you bad, it's Jesus. He willingly suffered on the cross for our eternal benefit. And I would venture to say that if the goodness of God is meant to lead one to repentance, then just maybe God desires to use your finite goodness towards your wife to point her to his infinite goodness in Christ, so that she might turn from her sin and trust Jesus as Savior and Lord, or obey him more fully, if she is a believer.

Love your wife without any conditions. And suffer nobly in your marriage for Christ Jesus. He is more than worth it.

www.ingramcontent.com/pod-product-compliance
Lightning Source LLC
Chambersburg PA
CBHW021624270326
41931CB00008B/860